Where do I go fo[r]

What's the best and

frommers.travelocity.com

Frommer's, the travel guide leader, has teamed up with **Travelocity.com,** the leader in online travel, to bring you an in-depth, easy-to-use resource designed to help you plan and book your trip online.

At **frommers.travelocity.com**, you'll find free online updates about your destination from the experts at Frommer's plus the outstanding travel planning and purchasing features of Travelocity.com. Travelocity.com provides reservations capabilities for 95 percent of all airline seats sold, more than 47,000 hotels, and over 50 car rental companies. In addition, Travelocity.com offers more than 2,000 exciting vacation and cruise packages. Travelocity.com puts you in complete control of your travel planning with these and other great features:

> **Expert travel guidance from Frommer's** - over 150 writers reporting from around the world!

> **Best Fare Finder** - an interactive calendar tells you when to travel to get the best airfare

> **Fare Watcher** - we'll track airfare changes to your favorite destinations

> **Dream Maps** - a mapping feature that suggests travel opportunities based on your budget

> **Shop Safe Guarantee** - 24 hours a day / 7 days a week live customer service, and more!

Whether traveling on a tight budget, looking for a quick weekend getaway, or planning the trip of a lifetime, Frommer's guides and Travelocity.com will make your travel dreams a reality. You've bought the book, now book the trip!

A New Star-Rating System & Other Exciting News from Frommer's!

In our continuing effort to publish the savviest, most up-to-date, and most appealing travel guides available, we've added some great new features.

Frommer's guides now include a new star-rating system. Every hotel, restaurant, and attraction is rated from 0 to 3 stars to help you set priorities and organize your time.

We've also added seven brand-new features that point you to the great deals, in-the-know advice, and unique experiences that separate travelers from tourists. Throughout the guide look for:

Finds	Special finds—those places only insiders know about
Fun Fact	Fun facts—details that make travelers more informed and their trips more fun
Kids	Best bets for kids—advice for the whole family
Moments	Special moments—those experiences that memories are made of
Overrated	Places or experiences not worth your time or money
Tips	Insider tips—some great ways to save time and money
Value	Great values—where to get the best deals

Frommer's®

P O R T A B L E

Disneyland®

1st Edition

by Stephanie Avnet Yates

Hungry Minds™

Best-Selling Books • Digital Downloads • e-Books
Answer Networks • e-Newsletters • Branded Web Sites • e-Learning
New York, NY • Cleveland, OH • Indianapolis, IN

ABOUT THE AUTHOR

A native of Los Angeles and an avid traveler, antiques hound, and pop history enthusiast, **Stephanie Avnet Yates** believes that California is best seen from behind the wheel of a little red convertible. Stephanie has authored *Frommer's Los Angeles* and *Frommer's Wonderful Weekends from Los Angeles*, and cowritten *Frommer's California*, in addition to contributing to several other regional guidebooks and websites. Online, she can be reached directly at savvy_girl@hotmail.com.

Published by:

HUNGRY MINDS, INC.

909 Third Ave.
New York, NY 10022

ISBN 0-7645-6463-3
ISSN 1534-9098

Editor: Kathleen Warnock
Production Editor: Ian Skinnari
Cartographer: Nicholas Trotter
Photo Editor: Richard Fox
Production by Hungry Minds Indianapolis Production Services

SPECIAL SALES

For general information on Hungry Minds' products and services, please contact our Customer Care department; within the U.S. at 800-762-2974, outside the U.S. at 317-572-3993 or fax 317-572-4002. For sales inquiries and reseller information, including discounts, bulk sales, customized editions, and premium sales, please contact our Customer Care department at 800-434-3422.

Manufactured in the United States of America

5 4 3 2 1

Contents

List of Maps

An Invitation to the Reader

In researching this book, we discovered many wonderful places—hotels, restaurants, shops, and more. We're sure you'll find others. Please tell us about them, so we can share the information with your fellow travelers in upcoming editions. If you were disappointed with a recommendation, we'd love to know that, too. Please write to:

Frommer's Portable Disneyland, 1st Edition
Hungry Minds, Inc. • 909 Third Avenue • New York, NY 10022

An Additional Note

Please be advised that travel information is subject to change at any time—and this is especially true of prices. We therefore suggest that you write or call ahead for confirmation when making your travel plans. The authors, editors, and publisher cannot be held responsible for the experiences of readers while traveling. Your safety is important to us, however, so we encourage you to stay alert and be aware of your surroundings. Keep a close eye on cameras, purses, and wallets, all favorite targets of thieves and pickpockets.

What the Symbols Mean

The following abbreviations are used for credit cards:

AE	American Express	DISC	Discover	V	Visa
DC	Diners Club	MC	MasterCard		

FROMMERS.COM

Now that you have the guidebook to a great trip, visit our website at www.frommers.com for travel information on nearly 2,000 destinations. With features updated regularly, we give you instant access to the most current trip-planning information available. At Frommers.com, you'll also find the best prices on airfares, accommodations, and car rentals—and you can even book travel online through our travel booking partners. At Frommers.com, you'll also find the following:

- Daily Newsletter highlighting the best travel deals
- Hot Spot of the Month/Vacation Sweepstakes & Travel Photo Contest
- More than 200 Travel Message Boards
- Outspoken Newsletters and Feature Articles on travel bargains, vacation ideas, tips & resources, and more!

Here's what critics say about Frommer's:

"Amazingly easy to use. Very portable, very complete."

—*Booklist*

"The only mainstream guide to list specific prices. The Walter Cronkite of guidebooks—with all that implies."

—*Travel & Leisure*

"Complete, concise, and filled with useful information."

—*New York Daily News*

"Hotel information is close to encyclopedic."

—*Des Moines Sunday Register*

"Detailed, accurate, and easy-to-read information for all price ranges."

—*Glamour Magazine*

The Best of Disneyland

There are newer and larger Disneyland parks in Florida, Tokyo, and even France, but the original and inspiration for all of them still opens its gates in Anaheim, California every day, proudly proclaiming itself "the Happiest Place on Earth." Smaller than Walt Disney World, Disneyland has always capitalized on being the world's first family-oriented mega theme park. Nostalgia is a big part of the original park's appeal, and despite many advancements, changes, and expansions over the years, Disneyland remains true to the vision of founder Walt Disney.

In 2001, Disney unveiled a brand-new theme park (California Adventure), a new shopping/dining/entertainment district (Downtown Disney), and a third on-site hotel (Disney's California Adventure). They also revamped their own name to "The Disneyland Resort," reflecting an expanded array of entertainment options. What does this all mean for you? Well, first of all, you'll probably want to think seriously about budgeting more time (and yes, more money) for your Disney visit—you'll need at least 3 full days to see it all. If you have limited time, plan carefully so you don't skip what's important to you. In the pages ahead we'll describe what to expect throughout the new Resort. There's lots of new stuff to check out, and we'll give you the lowdown on the best of what's new as well as the classic Disneyland experience.

1 Frommer's Favorite Disney Experiences

- **Riding the Monorail Around the Resort:** For an up-close-and-personal overview of the entire Disneyland area, climb aboard the Monorail for a short but scenic tour. Once envisioned as the prototype for the future of public transportation, the groovy 1960s monorail was a much-missed feature when it closed for construction of California Adventure (where it now glides across a scale replica of the Golden Gate Bridge). Die-hard fans always try for a seat inside the domed "bubble" cars at either end. See chapter 6, "What to See and Do at the Disneyland Resort."

- **Getting a Bird's Eye View from the Maliboomer:** If you've got the nerve to climb aboard this sky-high thrill ride in California Adventure, you'll be rewarded with a panoramic view of Disneyland, Anaheim, neighboring Garden Grove . . . right before beginning a jerky, free-fall descent back to earth. See chapter 6, "What to See and Do at the Disneyland Resort."

- **Standing in Line for the Haunted Mansion, Space Mountain, or Indiana Jones Adventure:** What's so fun about standing in line? Disney Imagineers (the in-house term for the people who create the attractions) have extended the atmosphere of the attractions to the waiting areas; while you're in line for the Haunted Mansion, you're surrounded by a groovy graveyard; intergalactic spaceport halls (Space Mountain), and hieroglyph-festooned jungle ruins (Indiana Jones Adventure). See chapter 6, "What to See and Do at the Disneyland Resort."

- **Visiting Disneyland at Christmastime:** Normally a pleasant postcard of bygone Americana, Main Street U.S.A. really pulls out the stops at holiday time. Cheerful lights twinkle at sundown, and a surprise "snowfall" (achieved with startlingly realistic opaque bubbles) follows the nightly fireworks spectacular. See chapter 6, "What to See and Do at the Disneyland Resort."

- **Watching the Candy Makers at Main Street's Candy Kitchen:** Being an apron-clad Disney candy-maker has to be one of the sweetest jobs in town, and you can watch them at work in an exhibition kitchen filled with enormous copper vats, marble work tables, taffy-pulling hooks, and other tools of the trade. Afterward, sample a caramel apple, fresh fudge, candy cane, or one of the many other old-fashioned varieties in the shop. See chapter 6, "What to See and Do at the Disneyland Resort."

- **The "Art of the Craft" Tour of the Grand Californian Hotel:** Even a casual glance will tell you the Craftsman-style interiors of Disney's newest—and most elegant—hotel bear the mark of experienced artisans. Offered daily and led by senior members of the hotel staff, these architecture and design tours reveal the story behind the style, and point out fascinating details. See chapter 4, "Accommodations."

- **"Soarin' Over California" at California Adventure:** Within days of the new park's opening, Disney staffers and early visitors all agreed that Soarin' Over California was the most thrilling of the new rides. Featuring years-in-development engineering, a high-tech lifelike surround film, and startling realistic surprise touches (you don't expect us to give anything away, do you?), the ride noiselessly sweeps riders through a virtual hang-gliding tour of the Golden State. See chapter 6, "What to See and Do at the Disneyland Resort."

- **Getting Your Name Stitched on Mouse Ears:** It's been a tradition since the early days of Disneyland, and kids still love getting their own Mickey or Minnie ears from stores with names like "The Mad Hatter" and "Hatmosphere." If your millinery taste dictates another style, choices range from a 3-cornered pirate hat to a Donald Duck-billed visor. See chapter 6, "What to See and Do at the Disneyland Resort."

2 Best Hotel Bets Around the Disneyland Resort

For full listings on all the lodgings listed below, see chapter 4, "Accommodations."

- **Best Hotel For Families:** Since family travelers are a huge part of the Anaheim area's economy, you can count on kids being well accommodated nearly everywhere. Hotels that offer special underage perks include **Portofino Inn & Suites,** 1831 S. Harbor Blvd., Anaheim (℗ **888/297-7143** or 714/782-7600), whose "Kid's Suites" offer kids their own room with bunk beds and a separate TV; the **Anabella Hotel,** 1030 W. Katella Ave., Anaheim (℗ **800/863-4888** or 714/905-1050), which also features bunk-bedded "Kid's Suites" with separate bedrooms plus a Sony Playstation for after-Disney entertainment; and the **Holiday Inn Hotel & Conference Center,** 7000 Beach Blvd., Buena Park (℗ **800/465-4329** or 714/522-7000), whose chain-wide families-welcome policies include free meals for the under-12 set, plus a tot-friendly wading pool.

- **Best Swimming Pool:** Since you can't swim in the lakes and lagoons in the Disney theme parks, which are designed for show, not for taking a plunge, the **Disneyland Hotel,** 1150 Magic Way, Anaheim (℗ **714/956-MICKEY** or 714/778-6600) offers a swimmable tropical island fantasy of pools, waterfalls, and white-sand beaches in the center of the hotel complex.

- **Most Convenient for Touring the Parks:** You can't get any closer to the action than at **Disney's Grand Californian,**

1600 So. Disneyland Dr., Anaheim (✆ **714/956-MICKEY** or 714/635-2300), which offers views into California Adventure (plus a guests-only entrance gate), easy access to the shops and restaurants of Downtown Disney, and is a short walk away from Disneyland's main gate. No monorails or shuttles needed—this is the heart of the Resort!

- **Best Value:** The charming **Candy Cane Inn,** 1747 S. Harbor Blvd., Anaheim (✆ **800/345-7057** or 714/774-5284) is a motel with class, one whose bargain rates don't mean you won't get treated with a personal touch. That same thoughtfulness went into the finely landscaped and invitingly furnished property, which features delightful swimming pools and a deal-enhancing free breakfast each morning.

- **Best Hotel at the Beach:** When you want easy access to the fun and games of Disney, but can't bear forsaking the beach's refreshing breeze, head for the intimate **Portofino Beach Hotel,** 2306 W. Ocean Front, Newport Beach (✆ **949/673-7030).** This boutique inn has an Old World flair and a prime Newport location steps from the sand—yet Anaheim is freeway close.

- **Best Health Club:** The **Westin South Coast Plaza**, 686 Anton Blvd., Costa Mesa (✆ **888/625-5144** or 714/540-2500) leads the pack in business traveler amenities, including a full-service fitness center. With state-of-the-art exercise machines, the center is complemented by a full service spa for soothing those post-workout kinks.

3 Best Dining Bets Around the Disneyland Resort

- **Best Dining for Kids:** It's a given that all the restaurants at the Disneyland Resort (in the parks, hotels, and Downtown Disney) are well-versed in serving pint-sized diners—count on kids' menus, booster and highchairs, and a tolerant attitude toward youthful exuberance. But **Goofy's Kitchen,** in the Disneyland Hotel (✆ **714/956-6755**) is a place *just* for them, where grown-ups take a backseat to kooky cartoon decor, kid-pleasing buffet fare, and tableside visits from Disney characters classic and contemporary. See p. 72 for a full listing.

- **Best Spot for a Romantic Dinner:** There's no contest . . . head for the elegant yet comfortable **Napa Rose** in Disney's Grand Californian Hotel (✆ **714/300-7170**), where fine-tuned wine country cuisine, respectful and professional service, and a warm Arts & Crafts atmosphere encourage romance. See if you can snag an outdoor table near the fire pit, and watch the sparks fly! See p. 70 for a full listing.

- **Best Value Meal:** You won't find it in the Disneyland Resort, where food-as-entertainment usually rules out bargain fare. But over at Knott's Berry Farm, **Mrs. Knott's Chicken Dinner Restaurant,** 8039 Beach Blvd., Buena Park (© **714/220-5080**) pays homage to its Depression-era roots with down home dinners that won't break the bank—and you don't even have to enter the park. See p. 78 for a full listing.
- **Best Outdoor Dining:** Under a vine-shaded trellis, the outdoor tables at **Naples Ristorante e Pizzeria** (© **714/776-6200**) comprise a large portion of the restaurant's seating, and offer a panoramic view of the Downtown Disney promenade and Disneyland's main gate. The ambiance is relaxed, with comfortable seating and unhurried service—Naples is a preferred lunch rendezvous for Disney corporate employees. See p. 73 for a full listing.
- **Best People-Watching:** The Uva Bar at **Catal Restaurant/ Uva Bar** in Downtown Disney (© **714/774-4442**) is actually not attached to its partner restaurant, but situated outdoors, behind a wrought-iron railing, in the center of the Downtown Disney shopping district, offering an excellent view of the human parade. Relax with wine and tapas and enjoy the promenade, European-style. Umbrellas shade you from the afternoon sun, while heat lamps diffuse evening's chill. See p. 72 for a full listing.

2

Planning Your Trip to the Disneyland Resort

Advance planning is the best way to avoid disappointment and make the most of your visit to the Disneyland Resort: By using the information in this chapter, you ensure you don't miss any essential attractions, avoid wasting any of your precious travel time, and get the best value for your vacation dollars. Helpful planning tips can also be found in chapter 4, "Accommodations" and chapter 6, "What to See and Do at the Disneyland Resort."

1 Visitor Information

For general information on the area, contact the **Anaheim/Orange County Visitor and Convention Bureau,** 800 W. Katella Ave. (© 714/765-8888; www.anaheimoc.org), who can fill you in on area activities and shopping. Be sure to request the *Official Visitors Guide* and the *Sunny Savings Coupon Book,* which contain discount offers from dozens of local attractions, hotels, restaurants, and shops. The Bureau is across the street from Disneyland inside the Convention Center, next to the dramatic cantilevered arena. It's open Monday to Friday from 8:30am to 5:30pm.

For information on **The Disneyland Resort**, including show schedules and ride closures that apply to the specific day(s) of your visit, call © 714/781-4565 (automated information) or 714/781-7290 (to speak to Guest Relations) or log onto www. disneyland.com.

Visitors spending time in Los Angeles proper can contact the **Los Angeles Convention and Visitors Bureau** (© 800/366-6116; Events Hotline 213/689-8822; www.lacvb.com), the city's main source for information. In addition to maintaining an informative Internet site and answering telephone inquiries, the Bureau provides two **walk-in visitor centers:** 685 S. Figueroa St., downtown (Monday through Friday from 8am to 5pm, Saturday from 8:30am to 5pm); and in Hollywood, at the historic Janes House, 6541 Hollywood Blvd. (Monday through Saturday from 9am to 5pm).

Many Los Angeles- and Orange County-area communities also have their own information centers, including the **Beverly Hills Visitors Bureau,** 239 S. Beverly Dr. (© **800/345-2210** or 310/271-8174; www.bhvb.org); the **West Hollywood Convention and Visitors Bureau,** 8687 Melrose Ave., #M-26 (© **800/368-6020** or 310/289-2525; www.visitwesthollywood.com); the **Santa Monica Convention and Visitors Bureau** (© **310/393-7593;** www.santamonica.com), whose Palisades Park walk-up center is located near the Santa Monica Pier, at 1400 Ocean Avenue; the **Newport Beach Conference & Visitors Bureau,** 3300 W. Coast Hwy. (© **800/94-COAST** or 949/722-1611; fax 949/722-1612; www.newportbeach-cvb.com); and the **Laguna Beach Visitors Bureau,** 252 Broadway (© **800/877-1115** or 949/497-9229; www.lagunabeachinfo.org).

ONLINE INFORMATION

As we mentioned above, one of the most useful sites to visit is the Anaheim/Orange County Visitor and Convention Bureau's official website at **www.anaheimoc.org**. In addition to updated information on area attractions and special events, you can download and print their Sunny Savings coupons (see above) directly from the site. Culture vultures searching for a local fix can check out **www.ocartsnet.org** for the latest on performing, visual, and fine arts events throughout Orange County. The local newspaper, *The Orange County Register* offers current events and local weather updates at **www.ocregister.com**.

You can also find out everything you need to know about the Disneyland Resort online, beginning with the official site, **www.disneyland.com**, which contains the latest information on park improvements and additions, plus special offers (sometime on airfare or reduced admission) and an interactive trip planner that lets you build a custom Disney vacation package.

Finally, the state of California has an official Travel & Tourism site at **www.gocalif.ca.gov**, that includes information on Disneyland and Southern California—plus plenty more on the Golden State.

WHEN TO GO

For some, the best time to visit the Disneyland Resort will be when *you* have vacation from work—and the kids are out of school. If

Southern California at a Glance

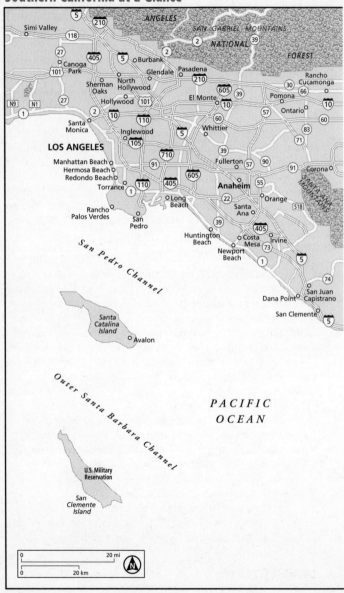

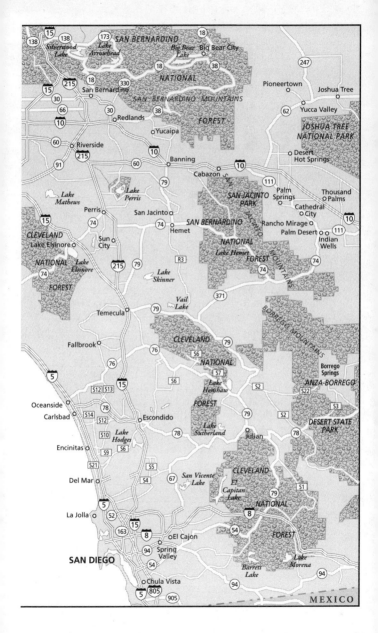

(Tips Preparing for a Day at Disneyland

A pre-vacation run through of this quick packing checklist can help you avoid common theme park pitfalls—and remember that these tips also apply to other Southern California family attractions like Universal Studios and LEGOLAND:

- Wear your most comfortable walking shoes, whether or not they go with your outfit. Unless you're in a stroller or wheelchair, you'll spend many hours walking, standing, and putting lots of strain on your legs and feet. Running or tennis shoes are the best; open-toed shoes are fine—especially on hot days—just make sure they will support your feet and have impact-cushioning soles.

- Expect a dramatic temperature drop after dark, even in summer. Bring a sweatshirt or jacket, perhaps even long pants; you can store them in a locker, leave them in the car, or tote them in a backpack. Too many visitors have shown up in shorts and tank tops, only to discover by 10pm they're freezing their buns off!

- Anything you might forget is available for purchase inside Disneyland and California Adventure—but you'll cringe at the marked-up prices. Do remember to bring your own sunscreen (the parks get a lot of direct sun); camera film (more than you think you'll want) and spare batteries; extra baby supplies; bottled water (or a sports bottle you can refill at drinking fountains); and snacks (if the kids get hungry in line, or you just balk at the concession prices).

you're flexible, though, a number of factors can influence your decision, because Disneyland has seasons of its very own:

- Strictly speaking, **Disneyland is busiest** in **summer** (between Memorial Day and Labor Day), on **holidays** (Thanksgiving week, Christmas week, President's Day weekend, Easter week, and Japan's "Golden Week" in early May), plus **weekends** year-round. All other periods are considered "off-season."
- If you want to **see all the shows/parades,** you'll have to come during the above high season, since scheduling is sporadic on

off-season weekdays. Disneyland's famed **fireworks** display *only* happens in summer. During the busy summertime, Tuesday through Thursday is the best time to come, and Friday and Saturday are the most crowded days.

- If your goal is to **avoid crowds and ride as many rides as possible,** visit on a weekday, preferably during November, December, or January (excluding Thanksgiving and Christmas weeks). Remember that fewer shows are scheduled, and you run the risk of some rides (never more than 3 or 4 at a time) being closed for maintenance, but this is the way to maximize a single day at the Park.

- If the Park is **open late** (past 10pm), you'll know they're expecting larger crowds—and so should you. On summer weekends, for example, Disneyland doesn't close till midnight or 1am. If closing time is early, crowds will probably be light; on off-season weekdays, the Park rarely stays open past 6 or 7 in the evening.

- Consider the **summer heat** in your decision . . . scorching days in July, August, and September can make waiting to get on a ride feel like a death march—with everyone crowding into available shady spots, and super-long lines to buy cold drinks. It's OK to visit during these times, just plan on plenty of rest time (take advantage of the indoor attractions) during the midday heat. Your reward later on will be a pleasantly balmy evening, when being outdoors becomes a delight.

- Worried about **rain?** Southern California gets most of its precipitation between January and April; but only a sustained downpour should affect your Disney plans. If you expect rain, bring both a collapsing umbrella and waterproof rain poncho (or splurge on the Mickey Mouse ponchos that suddenly appear throughout the Park when the first raindrop falls). A light drizzle will hardly affect your fun, and intermittent heavy showers can be managed by heading to indoor attractions or Downtown Disney's multiplex movie theater. Even if you get wet, you'll enjoy the lightest crowds of the year!

HOW MUCH TIME DO I NEED?

You'll want to devote *at least* one (very) full day to the Disneyland Resort, even if you're only going to take in one of the two theme parks. If you're planning to visit during one of the Park's peak periods (see above), crowds and wait times will limit the attractions

---

Tips   **Disneyland for International Visitors**

Visitors who require Disney information in other languages can call **Disneyland Resort Guest Relations** (© **714/781-7290**), where agents are available in French, German, Japanese, Spanish, and several other languages upon request. Once at the Resort, you'll find maps and guide brochures to Disneyland, California Adventure, and Downtown Disney printed in several languages. Currency exchange is available inside Disneyland at the **Bank of Main Street,** just inside the park entrance.

Web users can link to official Disney information sites in numerous languages at **www.disneyinternational.com**.

---

you're able to enjoy in a single day, so plan to spend the night and re-enter Disneyland fresh the following morning. Multi-day "Park Hopper" tickets (see "Essentials" in chapter 6) are a great deal for the money, and don't even require you to visit on consecutive days (if you want to break up your Disney stay with a day at the beach, for example). Families with small children will especially want to consider the multi-day option, regardless of the season; while it's a badge of honor for older kids (and younger grown-ups!) to survive a marathon Disney day, we all know that naptime crankiness will eventually rear its ugly head—regardless of whether you're in line for Mr. Toad's Wild Ride. So consider the factors of age and stamina level—along with assessing whether you need to see *absolutely everything* . . . or just a sampling—when you decide how many vacation days to devote to visiting the Resort.

Generally speaking, we suggest spending 2-3 days at the Disney attractions—that's enough to fully immerse yourself in the Resort's attractions and still leave some time (and hopefully some travel budget) for exploring more of Southern California.

If you're staying outside the Orange County area, but would like 2 days at the Park, plan on spending the night rather than driving back again the next day—you'll be glad you did.

If you're planning a once-in-a-lifetime trip, or Disneyland is the sole focus of your vacation, then 4-6 days will give you time to experience it all, including some non-Disney forays to nearby beaches, shopping, and cultural attractions.

SOUTHERN CALIFORNIA CALENDAR OF EVENTS

January

Tournament of Roses, Pasadena. A spectacular parade down Colorado Boulevard, with lavish floats, music, and equestrian entries, followed by the Rose Bowl football championship. Call *©* 626/449-4100 (www.tournamentofroses.com) for details, or just sit back and watch it on TV (you'll have a better view). January 1.

March

Los Angeles Marathon. This 26.2-mile run through the streets of Los Angeles attracts thousands of participants, from world champions to the guy next door; the big day also features a 5K run/walk and a bike marathon on the same route. The run starts in downtown Los Angeles. Call *©* 310/444-5544 or visit **www. lamarathon.com** for registration or spectator information. Early March.

April

Toyota Grand Prix, Long Beach. An exciting weekend of Indy-class auto racing and entertainment in and around downtown Long Beach, drawing world-class drivers from the United States and Europe, plus many celebrity contestants and spectators.

Tips Whale Watching

Each winter, pods of California gray whales making their annual migration from their Alaskan feeding grounds to breeding lagoons at the southern tip of Baja pass close by California shores; if you've ever been lucky enough to spot one of these graceful behemoths, you'll understand why whale watching is such an eagerly anticipated activity. From December through March, you can view this spectacular parade from land or sea. Recommended spots include **Point Vicente Lighthouse and Interpretive Center** (*©* 562/377-5370), on the windswept Palos Verdes Peninsula south of Los Angeles (about 45 minutes from Anaheim).

Boat excursions depart from a number of locations, including **Ventura Harbor** (Island Packers, *©* 805/642-1393; www. islandpackers.com) and **Newport Beach** (Newport Landing; *©* 949/675-0550; www.newportlanding.com).

Contact the Grand Prix Association at ✆ **888/82-SPEED** or 562/981-2600; www.longbeachgp.com. Mid-April.

Renaissance Pleasure Faire, San Bernardino. This annual event in the relatively remote Glen Helen Regional Park is one of America's largest Renaissance festivals. It features an Elizabethan-style marketplace with costumed performers and living history displays. The fair provides an entire day's activities, including shows, food, and crafts. You're encouraged to come in period costume. For ticket information, call ✆ **800/52-FAIRE** or 909/880-3911, or log onto the national web site **www. renaissance-faire.com**. Weekends from late April through Memorial Day.

May

Cinco de Mayo, Los Angeles. A weeklong celebration of Mexico's jubilant Independence Day takes place throughout the city. There's a carnival atmosphere with large crowds, live music, dancing, and food. The main festivities are held at El Pueblo de Los Angeles State Historic Park, downtown; call ✆ **213/628-1274** for information. Other events are held around the city. The week surrounding May 5.

June

Gay & Lesbian Pride Celebration, West Hollywood. An annual event for more than 30 years, this West Hollywood gathering just keeps getting larger. Outdoor stages, disco- and western-dance tents, food, and general revelry culminate in Sunday's flamboyant parade down Santa Monica Boulevard. Call ✆ **323/658-8700.** Last weekend in June.

July

Disneyland's Birthday, Anaheim. The anniversary of Disneyland's opening day falls each year, and the park usually celebrates with birthday celebrations, limited edition logo items, and special promotions. July 17.

Festival of Arts & Pageant of the Masters, Laguna Beach. A 60-plus-year tradition in artsy Laguna, this festival is built around a fantastic performance-art production in which live actors re-create famous Old Masters paintings. Other festivities include live music, crafts sales, art demonstrations and workshops, and the grassroots Sawdust Festival across the street. Grounds admission is $3; pageant tickets range from $15 to $40. Call ✆ **800/ 487-FEST** or 949/494-1145; there's online info at www.foapom. com. July through August.

August

Beach Festival, Huntington Beach. Two straight weeks of fun in the sun, featuring two surfing competitions—the US Open of Surfing and the world-class Pro of Surfing—plus extreme sports events like inline skating, BMX biking, skateboarding, and more. Includes entertainment, food, tons of product booths and giveaways—and plenty of tanned, swimsuit-clad bodies of both sexes. For more information, cal © **949/885-8200,** or log onto **www.hbvisit.com**. End of July.

September

Los Angeles County Fair, Pomona. Horse racing, arts, agricultural displays, celebrity entertainment, and carnival rides are among the attractions at one of the largest county fairs in the world. Held at the Los Angeles County Fair and Exposition Center; call © **909/623-3111** or visit **www.fairplex.com** for information. Throughout September.

October

Halloween Haunt at Knott's ScaryFarm, Buena Park. For almost 30 years Knott's has been replacing the tame "Berry" in its name with a spooky Halloween transformation that includes creepy "haunted" rides, eerie fun houses, roving monsters, ghouls, and goblins, and chilling effects not for the faint-hearted (or easily frightened children). Call the "Hauntline" at **& (714) 220-5200** or visit **www.halloweenhaunt.com.** Throughout October. See chapter 8 for more information on visiting Knott's.

November

Hollywood Christmas Parade. This spectacular, star-studded parade marches through the heart of Hollywood. For information call © **323/469-2337.** Sunday after Thanksgiving.

2 Tips for Travelers with Special Needs

FOR TRAVELERS WITH DISABILITIES

There are more resources than ever before for today's disabled traveler. *A World of Options,* a 658-page book for travelers with disabilities, covers everything from biking trips to scuba outfitters. It costs $45 (less for members) and is available from **Mobility International USA,** P.O. Box 10767, Eugene, OR 97440 (© **541/ 343-1284,** voice and TDD; www.miusa.org). Annual membership for Mobility International is $35, which includes their quarterly newsletter, *Over the Rainbow.*

You can join **Society for Accessible Travel & Hospitality** (SATH), 347 Fifth Ave., Suite 610, New York, NY 10016 (© 212/ 447-7284; www.sath.org), for $45 annually, $30 for seniors and students, to gain access to a vast network of connections in the travel industry. The Society provides information sheets on travel destinations and referrals to tour operators that specialize in travelers with disabilities. Its quarterly magazine, *Open World,* is full of good information and resources. A year's subscription is included with membership, or costs $18 ($35 outside the U.S.).

The **Los Angeles County Commission on Disabilities** (© 213/ 974-1053) provides telephone referrals and information about L.A. for the physically challenged.

Disney's official *Guidebook for Guests with Disabilities* is available at the wheelchair rental location and at information centers inside the parks. It's well worth picking up, and details accessibility issues for every area of Disneyland and California Adventure, and offers instructions on obtaining a Special Assistance Pass (SAP) based on your individual needs. The booklet also contains information on Braille guides and audiotape tours for the visually impaired, listening devices and written aids for the hearing impaired, and free sign language interpretation for Disney's live shows (an interpreter must be requested at least one week in advance).

Wheelchairs and Electric Convenience Vehicles (ECVs) can be rented at stations just inside the main entrance of each park; the daily fee is $7 for wheelchairs and $30 for ECVs. Both require a refundable deposit of $20 to rent, and you must be over 18.

Service animals are welcome in the parks, and must be kept leashed or harnessed at all times. The *Guidebook for Guests with Disabilities* contains a detailed list of rides on which service animals are *not* allowed, as well as those where Disney *recommends* they not be taken, although it's up to the owner's discretion; in either case, an attendant will wait at the end of the ride with your animal.

FOR FAMILIES

Several books offer tips on traveling with kids. *Family Travel* (Lanier Publishing International) and *How to Take Great Trips with Your Kids* (The Harvard Common Press) are full of good general advice. *The Unofficial Guide to California with Kids* (Hungry Minds, Inc.) is an excellent resource that covers the entire state. It rates and ranks attractions for each age group, lists dozens of family-friendly accommodations and restaurants, and suggests lots of beaches and activities that are fun for the whole clan.

Family Travel Times is published six times a year (℃ **888/822-4388** or 212/477-5524; www.familytraveltimes.com), and includes a weekly call-in service for subscribers. Subscriptions are $39 a year.

Parents can rent **strollers** for use inside the parks; the daily rental fee is $7. They're available at Disneyland just inside the Main Entrance, and in Tomorrowland at Star Trader. For California Adventure, rental stations are inside the Main Entrance in Golden Gateway, and across from Soarin' Over California at Fly 'n' Buy.

The **Baby Care Center,** located at the end of Main Street between the Camera Shop and First Aid, provides facilities for preparing formulas, warming bottles, nursing, and changing diapers. You can also find diaper machines and changing tables in many of Disneyland's restrooms. In California Adventure, there's a similarly outfitted Baby Center next to the Mission Tortilla Factory in the Pacific Wharf area.

FOR GAY & LESBIAN TRAVELERS

Many gay-oriented publications contain information and up-to-date listings, including *The Advocate,* a biweekly national magazine; *Frontiers,* a Southern California-based biweekly; and *Nightlife,* a local weekly with comprehensive entertainment listings, complete with maps. *Out and About* (℃ **800/929-2268;** www.outandabout. com), hailed for its "straight" and savvy reporting on gay travel, offers guidebooks and a monthly newsletter packed with good information on the gay and lesbian scene. Everybody from *Travel & Leisure* to the *New York Times* has praised the newsletter; a year's subscription costs $49.

The periodicals above are available at most newsstands citywide, and at **A Different Light Bookstore** (8853 Santa Monica Blvd., West Hollywood (℃ **310/854-6601;** www.adlbooks.com), L.A.'s largest and best gay-oriented bookshop. Their Web site is also enormously helpful.

The **International Gay & Lesbian Travel Association** (IGLTA; ℃ **800/448-8550** or 954/776-2626; www.iglta.org) links travelers with the appropriate gay-friendly service organization or tour specialist. With around 1,200 members, it offers quarterly newsletters, marketing mailings, and a membership directory that's updated quarterly.

FOR SENIORS

Nearly every attraction in Los Angeles offers a senior discount—even Disneyland, who defines seniors as 60 and over; age

Fun Fact Pride in the Parks

For years, Disneyland used to have a private party one night each year for gays and lesbians. Soon after the official event was cancelled, the "unofficial" version began taking shape. Modeled after a similar tradition at Walt Disney World in Orlando (Florida's Gay Day, held annually on the first Saturday after Memorial Day, which has now expanded to include other Orlando theme parks), the west coast event was dubbed **Gay Day 2** and usually takes place the first weekend in October (Saturday for **Disneyland**, Sunday for **California Adventure**). Since the event isn't supported by Disney—who will feign ignorance if asked for information—attendees don red shirts to identify each other and show the ever-increasing number of participants who attend each year (close to 15,000 people were expected for the 2001 Gay Day 2 weekend). The parks are open to the general public, so no special arrangements are required; however, you can find out more about simultaneous gay-only events, gay-friendly travel packages, and other useful information online at www.gayday2.com.

Gay and lesbian travelers headed to other Southern California theme parks should also note the following dates: **Gay Day** at **Knott's Berry Farm**, also an "unofficial" event, is held every year on the first Saturday in May. **Universal Studios Hollywood** has a **Gay Day** the first Saturday in August, and is the only theme park among the three to *officially* sponsor the event, which includes a separate-admission after-hours tea dance. You can get more information online at www.gaydayla.com, including information on how to purchase discounted admission tickets, a portion of which benefit AIDS Project Los Angeles. Red shirts are the garb of choice at these Gay Days, too.

requirements at different establishments can vary widely, with some as low as 50. Public transportation and movie theaters also have reduced rates. Don't be shy about asking for discounts, but always carry some kind of identification, such as a driver's license, that shows your date of birth. Also, mention the fact that you're a senior citizen when you first make your travel reservations. For example, both **Amtrak** (𝄪 **800/USA-RAIL**; www.amtrak.com) and **Greyhound** (𝄪 **800/752-4841**; www. greyhound.com) offer discounts to persons over 62.

Members of **AARP,** 601 E St. NW, Washington, DC 20049 (𝄪 **800/424-3410** or 202/434-2277; www.aarp.org), get discounts not only on hotels but on airfares and car rentals too. AARP also offers members a wide range of other special benefits, including *Modern Maturity* magazine and a monthly newsletter; membership is only $10 per year.

The Mature Traveler, a monthly 12-page newsletter on senior citizen travel, is a valuable resource. It is available by subscription ($30 a year) from GEM Publishing Group, Box 50400, Reno, NV 89513-0400. GEM also publishes *The Book of Deals,* a collection of more than 1,000 senior discounts on airlines, lodging, tours, and attractions around the country; it's available for $7.95 by calling 𝄪 **800/460-6676.** Another helpful publication is *101 Tips for the Mature Traveler,* available free from Grand Circle Travel, 347 Congress St., Suite 3A, Boston, MA 02210 (𝄪 **800/221-2610** or 617/350-7500; www.gct.com). Also check your newsstand for the quarterly magazine *Travel 50 & Beyond.*

FOR TRAVELERS WITH PETS

If you're thinking of taking Fido along to romp on a California beach, make sure you do some advance research. For one thing, dogs are restricted from most public beaches in Southern California, and leash laws apply in several communities. To find out where you can bring man's best friend, check out the online **Pets Welcome** service (www.petswelcome.com), which has national lists of accommodations that allow pets. The site also lists pet-related publications, medical travel tips, and links to other pet-related websites.

A good book to carry along is *The California Dog Lover's Companion: The Insider's Scoop on Where to Take Your Dog* (Publisher's Group West; 1998), a 900-page source for complete statewide listings of fenced dog parks, dog-friendly beaches, and other indispensable information.

Because pets are not allowed inside the Disney parks (or at the Disney Resort hotels), indoor **kennel** facilities are available for a charge of $10 per day (no overnight accommodations). The kennel is located to the right of the Main Entrance of Disneyland Park.

Value **The Art of the (Package) Deal**

If you intend to spend 2 or more nights in Disney territory, it pays to investigate the bevy of packaged vacation options available. Start by contacting your hotel (even those in Los Angeles or San Diego), to see whether they have Disneyland admission packages. Many vacation packagers include Disneyland and/or California Adventure (and other attractions) with their inclusive packages; independent fly/drive packages (no escorted tour groups, just a bulk rate on your airfare, hotel, and possibly rental car) are offered by **American Airlines Vacations** (© 800/321-2121; www.aavacations.com), **Continental Airlines Vacations** (© 800/634-5555; www.coolvacations.com), **Delta Vacations** (© 800/872-7786; www.deltavacations.com), **Southwest Airlines Vacations** (© 800/423-5683; www.swavacations.com), and **United Vacations** (© 800/328-6877; www.unitedvacations.com).

In addition to these airline agencies, travel package services are offered to American Express customers at **American Express Travel** (© 800/AXP-6898; www.americanexpress.com/travel), which books packages through various vendors, including Continental Vacations and Delta Vacations. Or contact **Liberty Travel** (© 888/271-1584; www.libertytravel.

3 Getting There

Los Angeles International Airport (© 310/646-5252; www.lawa.org/lax/laxframe.html), better known as LAX, is the region's major airport, about 30 miles away. Domestic airlines flying in and out of LAX include **Alaska Airlines** (© 800/252-7522; www.alaskaair.com), **America West** (© 800/235-9292; www.americawest.com), **American Airlines** (© 800/433-7300; www.aa.com), **Continental Airlines** (© 800/525-0280; www.continental.com), **Delta Air Lines** (© 800/221-1212; www.delta.com), **Northwest Airlines** (© 800/225-2525; www.nwa.com), **United Airlines** (© 800/241-6522; www.united.com), and **US Airways** (© 800/428-4322; www.usair.com).

The major rental car chains all have offices at LAX, including **Avis** (© 800/230-4898; www.avis.com), **Budget** (© 800/527-0700;

com), one of the oldest and biggest packagers; they offer great deals—with or without air—to the many popular California destinations, including San Diego and Disneyland.

And put a call in to the official Disney agency, **Walt Disney Travel Co.** (© **800/225-2024** or 714/520-5050). You can request a glossy catalog by mail, or log onto **www. disneyland.com** and click on "Book Your Vacation" to peruse package details, take a virtual tour of participating hotel properties, and get online price quotes for customized, date-specific packages. Hotel choices range from the official Disney hotels to one of 35 "neighbor hotels" in every price range (economy to superior) and category (from motel to all-suite); a range of available extras including admission to other Southern California attractions and tours (like Universal Studios, or a Tijuana shopping spree), and behind-the-scenes Disneyland tours, in a multitude of combinations.

Each official package includes multi-day admission, early park entry, free parking (at the Disney hotels), souvenirs, and Southern California coupon books. Rates are competitive with non-Disney packages, considering the extras.

www.budgetrentacar.com), **Enterprise** (© **800/325-8007;** www. enterprise.com), **Hertz** (© **800/654-3131;** www.hertz.com), and **National Car Rental** (© **800/CAR-RENT;** www.nationalcar. com).

To reach the Disneyland Resort by car from LAX, take I-105 east to I-605 north, then I-5 south; dedicated off ramps lead to the attraction's parking lots, hotels, and surrounding streets. For the lowdown on stowing your car, see "Parking at the Disneyland Resort" in chapter 3 "Getting to Know the Disneyland Area."

If you'd rather fly directly into Anaheim, the nearest airport is **John Wayne Airport** (19051 Airport Way N., Anaheim; © **949/ 252-5200**; www.ocair.com), 15 miles from Disneyland at the intersection of I-405 and Calif. 55. Most national airlines and major rental car agencies serve the airport. To reach Anaheim from the airport, take Calif. 55 east, then I-5 north to the Disneyland exit.

You can also catch a ride with **American Taxi** (© **888/482-9466**), whose cabs queue up at the Ground Transportation Center on the lower level; reservations are not necessary. Expect the fare to Disneyland to cost about $26. For one or two travelers, though, it's more cost-effective to use **Super Shuttle** (© **800/BLUE-VAN**; www.supershuttle.com), which charges $10 per person to the Disneyland area; advance reservations are recommended, but not required. *Tip:* Before you pay for a taxi or shuttle service, check with your hotel and see if they offer airport transportation.

4 Planning Your Trip Online

With a mouse, a modem, and a certain do-it-yourself determination, Internet users can tap into the same travel-planning databases that were once accessible only to travel agents. Sites such as **Travelocity, Expedia,** and **Orbitz** allow consumers to comparison shop for airfares, book flights, find last-minute bargains, and reserve hotel rooms and rental cars.

But don't fire your travel agent yet. Although online booking sites offer tips and data to help you shop, they cannot endow you with the experience that makes a seasoned, reliable travel agent an invaluable resource, even in the Internet age. And for consumers with a complex itinerary, a trusty travel agent is still the best way to arrange the most direct flights to and from the best airports.

Still, there's no denying the Internet's emergence as a powerful tool in researching and plotting travel time. The benefits of researching your trip online can be well worth the effort:

- **Last-minute specials,** known as "E-savers," such as weekend deals or Internet-only fares, are offered by airlines to fill empty seats. Most of these are announced on Tuesday or Wednesday and must be purchased online. They are only valid for travel that weekend, but some can be booked weeks or months in advance. Sign up for weekly e-mail alerts at airline websites (see page 20) or check megasites that compile comprehensive lists of E-savers, such as Smarter Living (smarterliving.com) or WebFlyer (www.webflyer.com).
- Some sites will send you **e-mail notification** when a cheap fare becomes available to your favorite destination. Some will also tell you when fares to a particular destination are lowest.
- The best of the travel planning sites are now **highly personalized;** they track your frequent-flier miles, and store your

Frommers.com: The Complete Travel Resource

For an excellent travel planning resource, we highly recommend **Arthur Frommer's Budget Travel Online** (www.frommers.com). We're a little biased, of course, but we guarantee you'll find the travel tips, reviews, monthly vacation giveaways, and online-booking capabilities thoroughly indispensable. Among the special features are: **"Ask the Expert"** bulletin boards, where Frommer's authors answer your questions via online postings; **Arthur Frommer's Daily Newsletter**, for the latest travel bargains and inside travel secrets; and Frommer's **Destinations archive**, where you'll get expert travel tips, hotel and dining recommendations, and advice on the sights to see for more than 200 destinations around the globe. Once your research is done, the **Online Reservation System** (www.frommers.com/booktravelnow) takes you to Frommer's favorite sites for booking your vacation at affordable prices.

seating and meal preferences, tentative itineraries, and credit-card information, letting you plan trips or check agendas quickly.

- All major airlines offer **incentives**—bonus frequent-flier miles, Internet-only discounts, sometimes even free cell phone rentals—when you purchase online or buy an E-ticket.
- Some airlines allow you to **purchase frequent-flier miles** on the Internet, by phone or by mail. It's worth investigating this option if you're within a couple thousand miles of award travel.
- Advances in mobile technology provide business travelers and other frequent travelers with **the ability to check flight status, change plans, or get specific directions** from hand-held computing devices, mobile phones, and pagers. Some sites will e-mail or page a passenger if a flight is delayed.

TRAVEL PLANNING & BOOKING SITES

The best travel planning and booking sites cast a wide net, offering domestic and international flights, hotel and rental-car bookings, plus news, destination information, and deals on cruises and vacation packages. Keep in mind that free (one-time) registration is often required for booking. Because several airlines are no longer willing to pay commissions on tickets sold by online travel agencies, be aware that these online agencies will either charge a $10 surcharge if you book a ticket on that carrier—or neglect to offer those air carriers' offerings.

The sites in this section are not intended to be a comprehensive list, but rather a discriminating selection to help you get started. Recognition is given to sites based on their content value and ease of use and is not paid for—unlike some website rankings, which are based on payment. Remember: This is a press-time snapshot of leading websites—some undoubtedly will have evolved or moved by the time you read this.

- **Travelocity** (www.travelocity.com or www.frommers. travelocity.com) and **Expedia** (www.expedia.com) are the most longstanding and reputable sites, each offering excellent selections and searches for complete vacation packages. Travelers search by destination and dates coupled with how much they are willing to spend.
- The latest buzz in the online travel world is about **Orbitz** (www.orbitz.com), a site launched by United, Delta, Northwest, American, and Continental airlines. It shows all possible fares for your desired trip, offering fares lower than those available through travel agents. (Stay tuned: At press time, travel-agency associations were waging an antitrust battle against this site.)
- **Qixo** (www.qixo.com) is another powerful search engine that allows you to search for flights and hotel rooms on 20 other travel-planning sites (such as Travelocity) at once. Qixo sorts results by price, after which you can book your travel directly through the site.

SMART E-SHOPPING

The savvy traveler is one who arms himself with good information. Here are a few tips to help you navigate the Internet successfully and safely.

- **Know when sales start.** Last-minute deals may vanish in minutes. If you have a favorite booking site or airline, find out when last-minute deals are released to the public. (For example, Southwest's specials are posted every Tuesday at 12:01am central time.)

- **Shop around.** Compare results from different sites and airlines—and against a travel agent's best fare, if you can. If possible, try a range of times and alternate airports before purchasing.
- **Follow the rules of the trade.** Book in advance, and choose an off-peak time and date if possible. Some sites tell you when fares to a destination tend to be cheapest.
- **Stay secure.** Book only through secure sites (some airline sites are not secure). Look for a key icon (Netscape) or a padlock (Internet Explorer) at the bottom of your Web browser before you enter credit card information or other personal data.
- **Avoid online auctions.** Sites that auction airline tickets and frequent-flier miles are the number-one perpetrators of Internet fraud, according to the National Consumers League.
- **Maintain a paper trail.** If you book an E-ticket, print out a confirmation, or write down your confirmation number, and keep it safe and accessible—or your trip could be a virtual one!

ONLINE TRAVELER'S TOOLBOX

Veteran travelers usually carry some essential items to make their trips easier. Following is a selection of online tools to bookmark and use.

- **Visa ATM Locator** (www.visa.com) or **MasterCard ATM Locator** (www.mastercard.com). Find ATMs in hundreds of cities in the U.S. and around the world.
- **Foreign Languages for Travelers** (www.travlang.com). Learn basic terms in more than 70 languages and click on any underlined phrase to hear what it sounds like. *Note:* Speakers and free audio software are required.
- **Intellicast** (www.intellicast.com). Weather forecasts for all 50 states and cities around the world. *Note:* Temperatures are in Celsius for many international destinations.
- **Mapquest** (www.mapquest.com). This best of the mapping sites lets you choose a specific address or destination, and in seconds, it returns a map and detailed directions.
- **Cybercafes.com** (www.cybercafes.com) or **Net Café Guide** (www.netcafeguide.com/mapindex.htm). Locate Internet cafes at hundreds of locations around the globe. Catch up on your e-mail and log onto the Web for a few dollars per hour.
- **Universal Currency Converter** (www.xe.net/currency). See what your dollar or pound is worth in more than 100 other countries.

Getting to Know
the Disneyland Area

The area surrounding the Disneyland Resort is a visitor and family mecca, so you should feel completely comfortable—and there's almost always someone around to provide assistance when you need it. In this chapter, we will familiarize you with the region around the resort, as well as where you might be staying in the Los Angeles area. We also provide practical advice for getting around and helpful facts and phone numbers you might need during your stay.

1 Orientation

VISITOR INFORMATION CENTERS

As mentioned in the previous chapter, for general area information, contact the **Anaheim/Orange County Visitor and Convention Bureau,** 800 W. Katella Ave. (© **714/765-8888;** www.anaheimoc. org). The Bureau is across the street from Disneyland inside the Convention Center, next to the cantilevered arena. It's open Monday to Friday from 8:30am to 5:30pm.

The **Buena Park Convention and Visitors Office,** 6280 Manchester Blvd., Suite 103 (© **800/541-3953** or 714/562-3560; www.buenapark.com/cvo), provides specialized information on the area, including Knott's Berry Farm.

Visitors including L.A. in their plans can contact the **Los Angeles Convention and Visitors Bureau** (© **800/366-6116;** Events Hotline 213/689-8822; www.lacvb.com) or head for one of the two **walk-in visitor centers.** See chapter 2, "Planning Your Trip to the Disneyland Resort," for more information on official information/ tourist offices.

ONLINE INFORMATION SOURCES

Along with the official web sites listed in chapter 2, another excellent guide is **At L.A.'s** Web site at **www.at-la.com**; the site's precise search engine (one of our favorite tools) provides links to more than 60,000 sites relating to the entire L.A. area, including Orange county (plus several more surrounding counties).

You can also find out everything you need to know about the Disneyland Resort online, beginning with the official site, **www.disneyland.com**.

AREA LAYOUT

The Disneyland Resort is in Anaheim, located in Orange County south of Los Angeles. Though many who live in the county work in L.A. and consider the area a far-flung bedroom community of the larger metropolis, Orange County has a distinct personality and independent spirit of its own. Vast master-planned communities co-exist with charming relics of the small farming towns that once dotted the region, while at the water's edge a series of alluring beach towns range from chic and shiny to funky and low-key (see "Neighborhoods in Brief," below). To navigate around Orange County, or between Anaheim and Los Angeles, you'll want to familiarize yourself with the freeway system.

MAIN ARTERIES & STREETS

Disneyland is located just blocks from **I-5,** otherwise known as the "Golden State Freeway" or the "Santa Ana Freeway." It stretches down the center of the state, eventually reaching San Diego.

I-405, also known as the "San Diego Freeway," runs north-south through L.A.'s Westside, connecting the San Fernando Valley with LAX, then continuing into Orange County before forking together with I-5 in Irvine, about 12 miles south of Disneyland.

Calif. 55 is a shorter freeway, stretching only from a spot northeast of Disneyland to the ocean, but it makes for smooth sailing down to Costa Mesa, Newport Beach, and other spots near Anaheim.

The streets in Anaheim are laid out in a symmetrical grid; the Disneyland Resort is bordered on the north by **Ball Road** and on the south by **Katella Avenue.** To the east is **Harbor Boulevard,** home to many of the affordable hotels outside Disneyland; follow this main thoroughfare south, and you'll wind up in Costa Mesa. To the west is **Disneyland Drive,** known as West Street on either side of the Disney compound; along this newly landscaped street you'll find the official Disney hotels, parking lots, and tram stops.

NEIGHBORHOODS IN BRIEF
ORANGE COUNTY AREA

The sleepy Orange County town of Anaheim grew up around Disneyland. Now, even beyond the Park, otherwise unspectacular, sprawling suburbs have become a playground of family hotels and restaurants, and unabashedly tourist-oriented attractions—like in neighboring Buena Park, a fellow former farmland community whose most prominent draw is Knott's Berry Farm.

Located a short drive—but a world apart—from the Disneyland Resort, the city of **Orange** is a charming throwback to 19th-century small town Americana (a real-life "Main Street U.S.A."). This hidden enclave boasts antique shopping, attractive dining (see chapter 5, "Dining"), and a grassy town square to anchor it all.

Further toward the coastline, **Costa Mesa** is populated with business hotels, gleaming tech-company business parks, and the elegant and vast South Coast Plaza, a shopping mall that is an attraction in its own right.

Huntington Beach is probably the largest Orange Coast city, and has seen the most urbanization. To some extent, this has changed the old boardwalk and pier into a modern outdoor mall where cliques of kids coexist with families and the surfers who continue to flock here, drawn by Huntington's legendary place in surf lore (Hawaiian surfer Duke Kahanamoku brought the sport here in the 1920s).

The name **Newport Beach** conjures comparisons to Rhode Island's Newport, where the well to do enjoy seaside living with all the creature comforts. That's the way it is here, too, but on a less grandiose scale. From the million-dollar Cape Cod-style cottages on sunny Balboa Island in the bay to elegant shopping complexes like Fashion Island, this is where fashionable socialites, right-wing celebrities, and business mavens can all be found.

Laguna Beach, whose breathtaking geography is marked by bold elevated headlands, coastal bluffs, and pocket coves, is known as an artists' enclave, but the truth is that Laguna has became so *in* (read: expensive) that it's driven most of the bohemians *out.* Their legacy remains with the annual **Festival of Arts and Pageant of the Masters** (see "Southern California Calendar of Events," in chapter 2), as well as a proliferation of art galleries intermingling with high-priced boutiques along the town's cozy streets. In warm weather, Laguna Beach has an overwhelming Mediterranean-island ambiance, which makes *everyone* feel beautifully, idly rich.

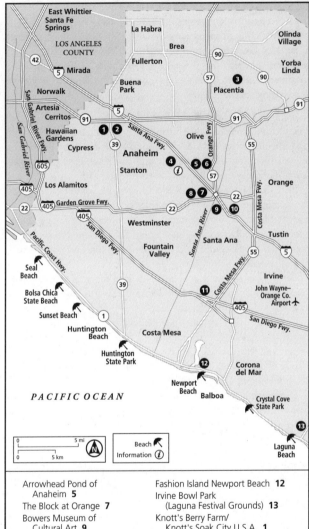

PACIFIC OCEAN

Beach 🏖️
Information ⓘ

0 ___ 5 mi
0 ___ 5 km

Arrowhead Pond of
  Anaheim **5**
The Block at Orange **7**
Bowers Museum of
  Cultural Art **9**
Crystal Cathedral **8**
Discovery Science Center **10**
The Disneyland Resort **4**
Edison Field **6**

Fashion Island Newport Beach **12**
Irvine Bowl Park
  (Laguna Festival Grounds) **13**
Knott's Berry Farm/
  Knott's Soak City U.S.A. **1**
Movieland Wax Museum **2**
Orange County Museum of Art **12**
Richard Nixon Library & Birthplace **3**
South Coast Plaza **11**

LOS ANGELES NEIGHBORHOODS

If you're considering choosing a Los Angeles hotel as your base—or simply planning to spend some time in L.A.—you'll want to have a sense of how this sprawling metropolis is organized, in order to maximize your time. This is not a complete listing of the L.A. neighborhoods, just the ones that correspond to those in chapter 4, "Accommodations."

L.A.'S WESTSIDE & THE BEACHES

Many visitors can't resist the lure of L.A.'s coastal communities—it's no coincidence the Westside is the ideal locale for many Angelenos as well. Boasting milder weather and less smog than inland, the towns along the coast all have a distinct mood and charm.

Pretty **Santa Monica** is L.A.'s premier beach community, known for its long ocean pier, artsy atmosphere, and somewhat-wacky residents. Shopping and dining are prime pastimes along Santa Monica's friendly streets—and in the Third Street Promenade, a pedestrian-only outdoor mall that's one of the country's most successful revitalization projects.

Venice was originally constructed with a series of narrow canals connected with quaint one-lane bridges. The area has lost some of that innocent charm over the years, and is still less affluent than neighboring Santa Monica, but gentrification is in full swing—bringing scores of great restaurants and boutiques, along with innovative and interesting modern architecture. Without a doubt, Venice is best known for its Ocean Front Walk, a nonstop circus of skaters, vendors, and colorful characters.

Brentwood, the world-famous backdrop to the O. J. Simpson melodrama, is really just a tiny, quiet, relatively upscale neighborhood with the typical L.A. mix of homes, restaurants, and strip malls. The Getty Center looms over Brentwood from its hilltop perch next to I-405.

Westwood, an urban village that the University of California at Los Angeles (UCLA) calls home, is bounded by I-405, Santa Monica Boulevard, Sunset Boulevard, and Beverly Hills.

Century City is a compact, busy, rather bland high-rise area sandwiched between West Los Angeles and Beverly Hills. It was once the back lot of 20th Century Fox studios. The primary draws here are the Shubert Theatre and the Century City Marketplace, a pleasant open-air mall.

West Los Angeles generally applies to everything that isn't one of the other Westside neighborhoods. It's basically the area south of

Santa Monica Boulevard, north of Venice Boulevard, east of Santa Monica and Venice, and west and south of Century City.

BEVERLY HILLS & HOLLYWOOD

The neighborhoods in the geographic center of the city are also those at the heart of its popularity. Most visitors like to base themselves here for easy access to L.A. sightseeing and entertainment.

Beverly Hills is roughly bounded by Olympic Boulevard on the south, Robertson Boulevard on the east, and Westwood and Century City on the west; it extends into the hills to the north. Politically distinct from the rest of Los Angeles, this famous enclave is best known for its palm tree-lined streets of palatial homes and high-priced shops. But it's not all glitz and glamour; the healthy mix of filthy rich, wannabes, and tourists that peoples downtown Beverly Hills creates a unique—and sometimes bizarre—atmosphere.

West Hollywood is a key-shaped community whose epicenter is the intersection of Santa Monica and La Cienega boulevards. Nestled between Beverly Hills and Hollywood, this politically independent town can feel either tony or tawdry, depending on which end of the city you're in. In addition to being home to some of the area's best restaurants, shops, and art galleries, West Hollywood is the center of L.A.'s gay community.

Hollywood itself, the center of which is Hollywood and Sunset boulevards (between La Brea and Vine), is the historic heart of L.A.'s movie industry. Visitors have always flocked to see landmark attractions such as the Walk of Fame and Mann's Chinese Theatre. Hollywood Boulevard is, for the first time in decades, showing signs of rising out of a seedy slump, with refurbished movie houses and stylish restaurants creeping back to the 'hood. By the time you visit, the centerpiece "Hollywood & Vine" complex will anchor the neighborhood, with shopping, entertainment, and a luxury hotel built around a new theater designed to host the Academy Awards.

THE SAN FERNANDO VALLEY

Known locally as "The Valley," this region was nationally popularized in the 1980s by the mall-loving "Valley Girl" stereotype. Snuggled between the Santa Monica and the San Gabriel mountain ranges, most of the Valley is residential and commercial and off the beaten track for tourists. But some of its attractions may draw you over the hill, such as Universal Studios Hollywood—and its trippy shopping and entertainment complex CityWalk (see chapter 8, "Other Southern California Family Attractions"). And you may make a trip to Burbank, west of these other suburbs and north of Universal City, to see one of your favorite TV shows being filmed at NBC or Warner Brothers Studios. There are also a few good restaurants and shops along Ventura Boulevard, in and around Studio City.

2 Getting Around

BY CAR

Do you really need a car to visit the Disneyland Resort? If visiting the theme park(s) and enjoying Disney's entertainment choices is your prime objective, then you probably do not. In addition, many area hotels offer shuttles to local shopping hotspots—and taxis are readily available for short hops within Orange County.

If, however, you're planning to base yourself in Los Angeles, or make several side trips outside of the Disney realm during your visit, you may want to consider the convenience of your own wheels.

RENTALS

Southern California is one of the cheaper places in America to rent a car. Major national companies usually rent Geo Metros, Ford Escorts, and similar vehicles for about $35 per day and $150 per week with unlimited mileage. All the major car-rental agencies have offices at John Wayne Airport and LAX; many of the larger hotels have rental desks in the lobby (especially helpful when you just want to rent for a portion of your stay—and few will impose a drop-off fee to return the vehicle to another Southern California office).

RENTERS INSURANCE

Before you drive off in a rental car, be sure you're insured. Assumptions about your personal auto insurance or a rental agency's additional coverage could end up costing you tens of thousands of dollars—even if you are involved in an accident that was clearly the fault of another driver.

If you already hold a **private auto insurance** policy in the United States, you are most likely covered for loss of or damage to a rental car and liability in case of injury to any other party involved in an accident. Be sure to find out whether you are covered in the area you are visiting, whether your policy extends to all persons who will be driving the rental car, how much liability is covered in case an out-side party is injured in an accident, and whether the type of vehicle you are renting is included under your contract. (Rental trucks, sport utility vehicles, and luxury vehicles or sports cars may not be covered.)

Tips **Saving Money on a Rental Car**

Car-rental rates vary even more than airline fares. The price you pay will depend on the size of the car, where and when you pick it up and drop it off, the length of the rental, where and how far you drive it, whether you purchase insurance, and a host of other factors. If you know you will need to rent a car (some tour packages include car rental), asking a few key questions could save you hundreds of dollars:

- Are weekend rates lower than weekday rates? Ask if the rate is the same for pickup Friday morning, for instance, as it is for Thursday night.
- Does the agency have a drop-off charge if you don't return the car to the location where you picked it up?
- Are special promotional rates available? If you see an advertised price in your local newspaper, be sure to ask for that specific rate; otherwise, you may be charged the standard cost. Terms change constantly. Also look for Internet-only rates or specials on the company's website or major travel booking sites.
- Are discounts available for members of AARP, AAA, frequent flyer programs, or trade unions? If you belong to any of these organizations, you may be entitled to discounts of up to 30%.
- How much tax will be added to the rental bill? Local tax? State use tax?
- How much does the rental company charge to refill your gas tank if you return with it less than full? Though most companies claim these prices are "competitive," fuel is almost always cheaper if you fill it yourself before you return the car. Some companies offer "refueling packages," where you pay for an entire tank of gas up front. The price is usually fairly competitive with local prices, but you don't get credit for any gas remaining in the tank. If a refueling stop on the way to the airport will make you miss your plane, then by all means take advantage of the fuel purchase option; otherwise, skip it.

Most **major credit cards** provide some degree of coverage as well—provided they were used to pay for the rental. Terms vary widely, however, so be sure to call your credit card company directly before you rent. The credit card will usually cover damage or theft of a rental car for the full cost of the vehicle, minus a deductible. (In a few states, however, theft is not covered; ask specifically about state law where you will be renting and driving.) If you already have auto insurance, your credit card will provide secondary coverage—which basically covers your deductible.

Credit cards will not cover liability, or the cost of injury to an outside party and/or damage to an outside party's vehicle. If you do not hold an insurance policy, you may want to consider purchasing additional liability insurance from your rental company. Be sure to check the terms, however: some rental agencies cover liability only if the renter is not at fault; even then, the rental company's obligation varies from state to state.

The basic insurance coverage offered by most car-rental companies, known as the **Loss/Damage Waiver (LDW)** or **Collision Damage Waiver (CDW),** can cost as much as $20 per day. It usually covers the full value of the vehicle with no deductible if an outside party causes an accident or other damage to the rental car. In all states but California, you will probably be covered in case of theft as well. Liability coverage varies according to the company policy and state law, but the minimum is usually at least $15,000. If you are at fault in an accident, however, you will be covered for the full replacement value of the car but not for liability. Some states allow you to buy additional liability coverage for such cases. Most rental companies will require a police report in order to process any claims you file, but your private insurer will not be notified of the accident.

Be sure to communicate any special needs in advance to the reservations agent. Most companies offer infant/child seats and vehicles equipped for drivers with disabilities. And many now offer cell phones with their cars—it's a good idea to consider. In addition to being invaluable for summoning help in case of an accident, they're also useful for calling for directions when you're lost and for getting roadside assistance in the event of mechanical difficulties.

PARKING AT THE DISNEYLAND RESORT

The Disneyland Resort's enormous parking structure on Disneyland Drive is difficult to miss; street signs are easy to see, and employees direct traffic to available spaces. Frequent shuttles carry passengers to Disney's main entrance, and to the Resort hotels. Parking is $7 per car for theme park visitors. Downtown Disney has its own lot and offers validated parking (3 hours free; 5 hours with restaurant or theater validation).

DRIVING RULES

In California, you may turn right at a red light after stopping unless a sign says otherwise. Likewise, you can turn left on a red light from a one-way street onto another one-way street after coming to a full stop. Keep in mind that pedestrians have the right-of-way at all times, so stop for people who have stepped off the curb. Also, California has a seat-belt law for both drivers and passengers, so buckle up before you venture out.

Many Southern California freeways have designated **carpool lanes,** also known as High Occupancy Vehicle (HOV) lanes or "white diamond" lanes (after the large diamonds painted on the blacktop along the lane). Some require two passengers, others three. Most on-ramps are metered during even light congestion to regulate the flow of traffic onto the freeway; cars in HOV lanes can pass the signal without stopping. Although there are tales of drivers sitting life-sized mannequins next to them in order to beat the system, don't consider ignoring the stoplights for any reason if you're not part of a carpool—fines begin at $271.

BY PUBLIC TRANSPORTATION
BY BUS

While extensive touring by bus is generally impractical, buses are an economical choice for short hops and occasional jaunts. Bus lines 43, 46, 50, and 205 serve the Disneyland Resort; the basic fare is $1 per boarding. Express routes 701 and 721 provide daily service between Orange County and Los Angeles; the fare is $3. For further assistance, including schedule information, contact the **Orange County Transit Authority** at © **714/636-RIDE** or log onto www.octa.net.

 ***FAST FACTS:* Anaheim & the Disneyland Resort**

American Express The most convenient Orange County office is located at 650 Anton Blvd. #A, Costa Mesa (© **714/ 540-3611**); there are also offices throughout Los Angeles, including 327 N. Beverly Dr., Beverly Hills (② 310/274-8277), and 8493 W. 3rd St., Los Angeles (②310/659-1682). To find additional locations in California, call ② 800/221-7282.

Area Codes   Within the past 20 years, Southern California has gone from having 3 area codes to over a dozen, with more promised by 2005. Even residents can't keep up with the changes. In Anaheim the area code is **714**; to the south (including Costa Mesa and Newport Beach) numbers begin with **949**. The Los Angeles area uses a whopping seven area codes, including **213**, **323**, **310**, **818**, **626**, and **562**. If it's all too much to remember, just dial ② **411** for information.

Babysitters   If you're staying at one of the larger hotels, the concierge can usually recommend a reliable babysitter, and several offer daytime or evening kids' programs (see chapter 4, "Accommodations"). If not, contact **Sitters Unlimited** (② **800/206-9066** or 909/734-6667).

Dentists   For a recommendation in the area, call the **Dental Referral Service** (② **800/422-8338**).

Doctors   Contact the **Uni-Health Information and Referral Hotline** (② **800/922-0000**) for a free, confidential physician referral.

Emergencies   For police, fire, or highway patrol, or in case of life-threatening medical emergencies, dial ② **911**.

Hospital   The nearest emergency room to the Disneyland Resort is **Western Medical Center,** 1025 S. Anaheim Blvd. (② 714/533-6220). In Los Angeles, head to centrally located Cedars-Sinai Medical Center, 8700 Beverly Blvd., Los Angeles (② 310/855-5000).

Kennels   Pets may be boarded near the Disneyland Resort at **Animal Inns,** 10852 Garden Grove Blvd., Garden Grove (② 714/636-4455; www.animalinns.com); for information on kennels at the Disney theme parks, see the section "For Travelers With Pets," in chapter 2, "Planning Your Trip to the Disneyland Resort."

Liquor Laws   Liquor and grocery stores can sell packaged alcoholic beverages between 6am and 2am. Most restaurants, nightclubs, and bars are licensed to serve alcoholic drinks during the same hours. The legal age for purchase and consumption is 21; proof of age is required. For availability of alcoholic beverages in the Disneyland Resort, see chapter 5, "Dining."

Lockers   See "Essentials" in chapter 6, "What to See and Do at the Disneyland Resort."

Lost Children   Disneyland and California Adventure each have a designated spot for parents to meet up with lost children (or any group members who become separated). Find out where it is when you enter, and instruct your children to ask park personnel to take them there if they're lost. Young children should have nametags that include their parents' names, the name of the hotel where they're staying, and a contact number back home in the very rare case that parents can't be located.

Newspapers/Magazines   The *Orange County Register* is Anaheim's primary local paper; many residents also get the *Los Angeles Times,* which publishes a daily Orange County edition. While *Coast* magazine covers area style and culture for affluent readers. *O.C. Weekly,* a free weekly listings magazine, is packed with information on current events around town. It's available from sidewalk news racks and in many stores and restaurants around the city.

Pharmacies   A 24-hour branch of **Sav-on Drugs** can be found about 5 miles from the Disneyland Resort at 1021 N. State College Blvd., Anaheim (✆ **714/991-8150**).

Police   In an emergency, dial ✆ **911.** For nonemergency police matters, call the Orange County Sheriff's Department (✆ **714/647-7000.**

Post Office   A branch of the United States Postal Service is located near Disneyland at 1180 W. Ball Rd., only about 3 blocks from the Disneyland Resort. For additional locations and information on hours and rates, call ✆ **800/ASK-USPS.**

Safety   Don't let Disneyland's gated ambiance and clean family atmosphere allow you to relax your guard, because distracted tourists can easily be the victims of pickpockets, muggers, and car thieves. Avoid carrying valuables with you on the street, and don't display expensive cameras or electronic equipment. It's a good idea to keep your valuables in a safe-deposit box, either at your hotel's front desk or in your room (if one is provided). Keep a close eye on valuables when you're in a public place—restaurant, theater, or airport terminal. Renting a locker is preferable to leaving your valuables in the trunk of your rental car, even in Disneyland parking lots. Be cautious when touring the parks, and avoid carrying large amounts of cash in a backpack or fanny pack, which could be easily accessed while you're standing in line for a ride or show. Hold onto your pocketbook, and place your billfold in an inside pocket.

If you're renting a car, read the safety instructions the rental company provides. If you drive off a highway into a doubtful neighborhood, leave the area as quickly as possible. If you have an accident, even on the highway, stay in your car with the doors locked until you assess the situation or until the police arrive. Always try to park in well-lit and well-traveled areas. Never leave any packages or valuables in sight. If someone attempts to rob you or steal your car, don't try to resist the thief or carjacker. Report the incident to the police department immediately by calling © **911**. This is a free call, even from pay phones. Remember that children should never ride in the front seat of a car equipped with air bags.

Taxes   **Sales tax** (including California state tax plus any local taxes) ranges from 7% to 8% throughout Southern California; hotel taxes also vary (see chapter 4, "Accommodations" for details).

Taxis   See "Getting Around," earlier in this chapter.

Time Zone   California is in the **Pacific** time zone, which is 8 hours behind Greenwich mean time and 3 hours behind Eastern time. Daylight Savings Time is observed.

4

Accommodations

Deciding to visit the Disneyland Resort is just the first step . . . next comes the search for accommodations. Choices abound, in every area—and every price range. Often, your decision will be influenced by price and availability, which vary seasonally (see "When to Go," in chapter 2). What's our number one piece of advice? Make your reservations as far in advance as possible, especially if you're visiting during a peak travel season or must stay within a strict budget.

We've organized our hotel choices below by area, beginning with those in and around the Disneyland Resort in Anaheim—including several choices elsewhere in Orange County, even some near the beach! Because many of you will consider a Disney visit as an "add-on" to your vacation in Los Angeles, we also offer suggestions for L.A.'s most accessible neighborhoods. Remember that all rates listed are "rack" rates, the hotel's published price *before* any discounts, special offers, or packages. And don't forget to factor in the hotel tax, which ranges from 8% to 17% throughout Southern California (each city has a different rate—for example, Anaheim's hotel tax is 15%, Newport Beach 10%).

1 Disneyland Area Accommodations

IN THE RESORT
VERY EXPENSIVE

Disney's Grand Californian Hotel ⊛⊛ *Kids*   Disney spared no detail when constructing this enormous version of an Arts and Crafts-era lodge (think Yosemite's Awhanee, Pasadena's Gamble House), hiring craftspeople throughout the state to contribute one-of-a-kind tiles, furniture, sculptures, and artwork. Taking inspiration from California's redwood forests, mission pioneers, and plein-air painters, designers created a nostalgic yet state-of-the-art high-rise hotel. Enter through subtle (where's the door?) stained-glass sliding panels to the hotel's centerpiece, a six-story "living room" with a William Morris-designed marble "carpet", angled

Saving on Your Hotel Room

In the listings below, we've tried to give you an idea of the kind of deals that might be available at particular hotels: which ones have the best discounted packages, which ones offer AAA and other discounts, which ones allow kids to stay with Mom and Dad for free, and so on. But there's no way of knowing what the offers will be when you're booking, so also consider these general tips:

- Don't be afraid to bargain. Always ask for a lower price than the first quote. Most rack rates include commissions of 10% to 25% or more for travel agents, which many hotels will cut if you haggle a bit. Ask politely whether a less-expensive room is available than the first one mentioned or whether any special rates apply to you. You might qualify for corporate, student, military, senior citizen, or other discounts. Always mention membership in AAA, AARP, frequent-flyer programs, corporate or military organizations, or trade unions, which might entitle you to special deals as well. The big chains tend to be good about trying to save you money, but reservation agents often won't volunteer the information; you'll have to dig for it.

- Coastal and resort hotels are most crowded and therefore most expensive on weekends, so discounts are often available for midweek stays. On the other hand, business and convention hotels (this includes most larger Disney-area hotels, since the Anaheim Convention Center is across the street from Disneyland) are busiest during the

skylight seen through exposed support beams, display cases of Craftsman treasures, and a three-story walk-in "hearth" whose fire warms Stickley-style rockers and plush leather armchairs. Guest rooms are spacious and smartly designed, carrying through the Arts and Crafts theme well considering the hotel's grand scale. The best rooms overlook California Adventure (but you'll pay for that view), which offers a shortcut entrance for hotel guests only. Despite the sophisticated, luxurious air of the Grand Californian, this is a hotel that truly caters to families, with a bevy of room configurations including one with a double bed plus bunk-beds-with-trundle.

week, while discounts tend to be abundant on weekends. Planning your vacation just before or after the peak summer season can mean big savings too. For more on travel seasons in Southern California and at Disneyland, see "When to Go," in chapter 2.

- Dial direct. When booking a room in a chain hotel, call the hotel's local line, as well as the toll-free number, and see where you get the best deal. The clerk who runs the place is more likely to know vacancies and will often grant discounts in order to fill up.

- Rely on a qualified professional. Certain hotels give travel agents discounts in exchange for steering business their way, so an agent can sometimes be better equipped to negotiate discounts for you.

- Look at package deals. In some cases, you'll get airfare, accommodations, transportation to and from the airport, plus extras—maybe even discounts on theme-park admission—for less than the price of the hotel if you booked it yourself. See the box called "The Art of the (Package) Deal," in chapter 2.

- Consider a suite. If you are traveling with your family, a suite can be a terrific bargain, as they're almost always cheaper than two hotel rooms, and usually feature sofa beds in the living room. Some places charge for extra adults (or older children) beyond two, some don't, so check.

Since the hotel provides sleeping bags (rather than rollaways) for kids, this standard-size room will sleep a family of six—but you have to share the bathroom.

1600 So. Disneyland Dr., Anaheim, CA 92802. © **714/956-MICKEY** (central reservations) or 714/635-2300. Fax 714/956-6099. www.disneyland.com. 751 units. $205-$335 double; from $345 suite. AE, DC, DISC, MC, V. Free self-parking; valet $6. **Amenities:** 3 restaurants; lounge; 2 outdoor pools; health club & spa; whirlpool; children's center; game room/arcade; concierge; business center; 24-hour room service; laundry/dry cleaning; concierge level rooms. *In room:* A/C, TV w/pay movies, dataport, minibar, coffeemaker, hair dryer, iron, bathrobes, safe, portable crib.

EXPENSIVE

The Disneyland Hotel ⟨⟨ *Kids*   The holy grail of Disneygoers has always been this, the "Official Hotel of the Magic Kingdom." A direct monorail connection to Disneyland means you'll be able to return to your room anytime, whether to take a much-needed nap or to change your soaked shorts after your Splash Mountain adventure. The theme hotel is an attraction itself, and the best choice for families with small children. The rooms aren't fancy, but they're comfortably and attractively furnished, like a good-quality business hotel, and all have balconies. In-room amenities include movie channels (with free Disney Channel, naturally) and Disney-themed toiletries and accessories. This all-inclusive resort offers over 10 combined restaurants, snack bars, and cocktail lounges; every kind of service desk; a fantasy swimming lagoon with white-sand beach; and video game center.

The complex includes the adjoining **Paradise Pier Hotel**, (a tower that at one time was an independent hotel. Several years ago the Disneyland Hotel took it over, and revamped it to match the Paradise Pier theme). It offers a Disney version of Asian tranquility; adults and older kids looking to escape the frenetically colorful Disney atmosphere will appreciate this option. It shares the pools and other recreation options with the Disneyland Hotel. Most important for many, hotel guests get to enter the park early almost every day and enjoy the rides before lines form. The amount of time varies from day to day, but usually you can enter 1½ hours early. Call ahead to check the schedule. When you're planning your trip, inquire about multiple-day packages that allow you to take on the park at your own pace and usually include free parking.

1150 Magic Way, Anaheim, CA 92802. © **714/956-MICKEY** (central reservations) or 714/778-6600 (Disneyland Hotel) or 714/999-0990 (Paradise Pier Hotel). Reservations fax 714/956-6582. 1,198 units. $170–$285 double; from $275 suite. AE, MC, V. Parking $10. **Amenities:** 10 restaurants; 3 lounges; 3 outdoor pools; health club; whirlpool; children's programs; game room; concierge; shopping arcade; salon; 24-hour room service; babysitting; laundry/dry cleaning. *In room:* A/C, TV w/pay movies, dataport, minibar, coffeemaker, hair dryer, safe.

OUTSIDE THE PARK
VERY EXPENSIVE

Sheraton Anaheim Hotel ⟨   This hotel rises to the festive theme-park occasion with its fanciful English Tudor architecture; it's a castle that lures business conventions, Disney-bound families, and local high school proms. The public areas are quiet and

Accommodations in the Disneyland Area

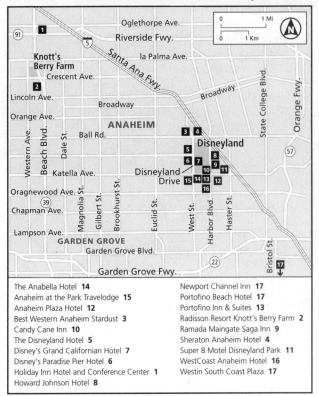

The Anabella Hotel **14**
Anaheim at the Park Travelodge **15**
Anaheim Plaza Hotel **12**
Best Western Anaheim Stardust **3**
Candy Cane Inn **10**
The Disneyland Hotel **5**
Disney's Grand Californian Hotel **7**
Disney's Paradise Pier Hotel **6**
Holiday Inn Hotel and Conference Center **1**
Howard Johnson Hotel **8**

Newport Channel Inn **17**
Portofino Beach Hotel **17**
Portofino Inn & Suites **13**
Radisson Resort Knott's Berry Farm **2**
Ramada Maingate Saga Inn **9**
Sheraton Anaheim Hotel **4**
Super 8 Motel Disneyland Park **11**
WestCoast Anaheim Hotel **16**
Westin South Coast Plaza **17**

elegant—intimate gardens with fountains and koi ponds, plush lobby and lounges—which can be a pleasing touch after a frantic day at the theme parks. The rooms are modern and unusually spacious, but otherwise not distinctive. A large swimming pool sits in the center of the complex, surrounded by attractive landscaping. Don't be put off by the high rack rates; rooms commonly go for $100 to $130, even on busy summer weekends.

1015 W. Ball Rd. (at I-5), Anaheim, CA 92802. ✆ **800/325-3535** or 714/778-1700. Fax 714/535-3889. 489 units. $190–$225 double; $290–$360 suite. AE, DC, MC, V. Parking $10; free Disneyland shuttle. **Amenities:** 2 restaurants; lounge; outdoor pool; fitness center; whirlpool; concierge; 24-hour room service; laundry/dry cleaning; coin-op laundry. *In room:* A/C, TV w/pay movies, dataport, minibar, coffeemaker, hair dryer, iron.

Is a Disney Hotel Right for You?

We'll admit it right off; the official Disney hotels are our favorites, both for convenience and ambiance. But there are lots of reasons to stay at one of the hotels and motels that line the surrounding blocks . . . not the least of which is that sometimes all 2,000-plus Disney guest rooms might be full! There are numerous hotels within easy walking distance of the Park, and all welcome families. If you're staying at a hotel in the immediate area, it's likely they'll offer a free Disney shuttle—either with their own van, or as a scheduled stop on the Park's shuttle. By all means, take advantage of it. Driving to and parking at the Park (see chapter 3, "Getting to Know the Disneyland Area") is perfectly easy for visitors coming from farther away, but an unnecessary extra step for folks staying close by.

Can't decide whether to stay "off-campus," or splurge on one of the official Disney hotels? The main advantages of going 100% Disney are:

- The Disney monorail, which circumnavigates the theme parks, also has a stop midway between all the official hotels—so when you get weary of hoofing it, simply hop aboard from within the Park and zip straight to your room (or the swimming pool!) Dedicated ticket booths and entry turnstiles at the monorail station mean you can also avoid the Disneyland main entrance crush. The Grand Californian even has its own gate into California Adventure for hotel guests only.
- All Disney Resort hotel guests get to enter Disneyland 1½ hours early, enjoying the major rides before long lines

EXPENSIVE

The Anabella Hotel   Uniting several formerly independent low-rise hotels across the street from California Adventure, the brand-new (in 2001) Anabella started from scratch, gutting each building to create carefully planned rooms for park-bound families and business travelers alike. The new complex features a vaguely Mission-style facade of whitewashed walls and red-tiled roofs, though guest room interiors are strictly contemporary in style and modern in appointments. Bathrooms are generously sized and form (be sure to wave to the patient folks roped off along Main Street). This shouldn't be your deciding factor, though, since packages from other hotels can also include the early admission feature.

- Hotel guests have charge privileges at all Disney Resort restaurants and stores. Plus, any purchases you make at the Disney parks or Downtown Disney shops can be delivered directly to your room at no extra charge, a value-added service that saves time and energy—no more schlepping souvenirs around the park, or putting off all your purchases until the exhausted end of the day.

On the other hand, more economical rooms can usually be found at the hotels lining the streets surrounding the Park. They may not be as much of a themed attraction as the Disney hotels, but when saving money is your prime concern, the "off-campus" hotels also have the following advantages:

- Free shuttles run frequently from the surrounding properties to the Park's main entrance, so you can enjoy the same in/out privilege that monorail riders do, though a bit more walking is necessary.
- There are no parking charges at most of the non-Disney hotels, and access to your car (and the freeway onramps) will be less complicated.
- Breakfast is often included in these room rates, a boon for budget-conscious families. If not, you can start the day at one of several inexpensive coffee shops (like Denny's, Millie's, or Coco's) just outside the Park, rather than feel obliged to spend more at a Disney restaurant.

outfitted in honey-toned granite; most have a tub-shower combo—just a few are shower-only. Though parking areas dot the grounds, you'll also find a pleasant garden around the central swimming pool and whirlpool; a separate adult pool hides out next to the street-side fitness room. Business travelers will appreciate the in-room executive desks with high-speed Internet access, while families can take advantage of "kids suites" complete with bunk beds and separate bedrooms. There's a pleasant indoor-outdoor all-day restaurant, and the hotel is a stop on both the Disney and Convention Center shuttle routes. *Note:* Rooms and rates vary wildly in terms of room size, layout, and occupancy limits; extra time spent with the reservationist will pay off in the most comfortable room for your needs.

1030 W. Katella Ave., Anaheim, CA 92802. © **800/863-4888** or 714/905-1050. Fax 714/905-1054. www.anabellahotel.com. 358 units. $159–$299 double. AE, DC, DISC, MC, V. Free parking. **Amenities:** Restaurant; lounge; 2 outdoor heated pools; whirlpool; exercise room; nail salon; concierge; activities desk; business center; room service (7am to 11pm); dry cleaning/laundry; self-service laundromat. *In room:* A/C, TV w/pay movies, Web TV, and Sony Playstation, dataport, fridge, coffeemaker, hair dryer, iron, safe.

WestCoast Anaheim Hotel ☆ Although this hotel, in the Anaheim Convention Center complex (across the street from the Disneyland Resort), draws primarily a business crowd, it has much to appeal to the leisure traveler. The contemporary, comfortable rooms in the 12-story tower all have balconies overlooking either the Disney theme parks or the hotel's luxurious pool area, which includes a sundeck, and snack and cocktail-bar gazebo. The front desk can provide fax machines and refrigerators upon request. The Old West frontier-themed restaurant serves steak and seafood along with a few colorful game selections.

1855 S. Harbor Blvd. (south of Katella Ave.), Anaheim, CA 92802. © **800/426-0670** or 714/750-1811. Fax 714/971-2485. www.westcoastanaheimhotel.com. 500 units. $195 double. Disneyland package available. AE, DC, DISC, MC, V. Self-parking $10, valet $13; free Disneyland shuttle. **Amenities:** 2 restaurants; 2 lounges; outdoor pool; fitness center; whirlpool; activities desk; car-rental desk; 24-hour business center; room service (6am to 11pm); laundry/dry cleaning. *In room:* A/C, TV w/pay movies and Sony Playstation, dataport, coffeemaker, hair dryer, iron.

MODERATE

Anaheim Plaza Hotel ☆ *(Value)* You can easily cross the street to the main Disneyland/California Adventure main gate, or take the Anaheim Plaza's free shuttle. Once you return, you'll appreciate the way this 32-year-old hotel's clever design shuts out the noisy world. In fact, the seven two-story garden buildings remind me more of 1960s Waikiki than busy Anaheim. The Olympic-size heated outdoor pool and whirlpool are unfortunately surrounded by Astroturf, and the plain motel-style furnishings are beginning to look a little tired. On the plus side, nothing's changed about the light-filled modern lobby, or the friendly rates, which often drop as low as $49.

1700 S. Harbor Blvd., Anaheim, CA 92802. © **800/228-1357** or 714/772-5900. Fax 714/772-8386. www.anaheimplazahotel.com. 300 units. $79–$150 double; from $185 suite. Rates include continental breakfast. AE, DC, DISC, MC, V. Free parking and Disney shuttle. **Amenities:** Restaurant; lounge; outdoor pool;

whirlpool; room service (8am to 11pm); laundry/dry cleaning; coin-op laundry. *In room:* A/C, TV, coffeemaker.

Portofino Inn & Suites ✿ *(Kids* Emerging from the multi-year rubble of the former Jolly Roger Hotel renovation, this brand-spanking new duo of high-rise all-suite buildings sports a cheery yellow exterior and family-friendly interior—just in time for the expanded Disneyland Resort. The location couldn't be better—directly across the street from California Adventure's backside, and they'll even shuttle you straight to the front gate. Designed to work as well for business travelers from the nearby Convention Center as for Disney-bound families, the Portofino offers contemporary, stylish furnishings as well as vacation-friendly rates and suites for any family configuration. We especially love the "Kid's Suite," which features bunk beds *and* sofa sleeper, plus TV, fridge, and microwave—and that's just in the kids' room; Mom and Dad have a separate bedroom with grown-up comforts like double vanity, shower massage, and their own TV.

1831 So. Harbor Blvd. (at Katella), Anaheim, CA 92802. ✆ **888/297-7143** or 714/782-7600. Fax 714/782-7619. 190 units. $94–$159 double; $109–$219 suite. Midweek, off-season, and other discounts available. AE, DC, DISC, MC, V. Free parking and Disneyland shuttle. **Amenities:** Restaurant; outdoor pool; fitness center; whirlpool; game room; tour desk; laundry/dry cleaning; coin-op laundry. *In room:* A/C, TV w/pay movies, dataport, coffeemaker, hair dryer, iron.

INEXPENSIVE

Best Western Anaheim Stardust Located on the back side of Disneyland, this modest hotel will appeal to the budget-conscious traveler who isn't willing to sacrifice everything. All rooms have a refrigerator and microwave, breakfast is served in a refurbished train dining car, and you can relax by the large outdoor heated pool and whirlpool while using the laundry room. The extra-large family rooms accommodate virtually any brood, and shuttles run regularly to the parks.

1057 W. Ball Rd., Anaheim, CA 92802. ✆ **800/222-3639** or 714/774-7600. Fax 714/535-6953. 121 units. $64–$89 double; $105 family room. Rates include full breakfast. AE, DC, DISC, MC, V. Free parking and Disney shuttle. **Amenities:** Restaurant; outdoor pool; whirlpool; self-service laundry. *In room:* A/C, TV, fridge.

Ramada Maingate Saga Inn *(Value* Though recent Disney construction has obscured the formerly imposing "main gate", this motel's name still indicates how enticingly close it is to the theme parks. It's a large property, with a vaguely Tudor castle exterior undoubtedly borrowed from Fantasyland. If you've still got energy after a day playing at the Disneyland Resort, the Ramada offers miniature golf, game arcades, and a branch of reliable Tony Roma's rib joint adjacent to the motel.

1650 S. Harbor Blvd., Anaheim, CA 92802. (© 800/854-6097 or 714/772-0440. Fax 714/991-8219. 185 units. $71–$108 double. Rates include continental breakfast. Kids 18 and under stay free. AAA discounts available; check also on www. ramada.com and ask about "Super Saver" rates, often as low as $58. AE, DC, DISC, MC, V. Free parking and Disney shuttle. **Amenities:** Restaurant; lounge; outdoor heated pool; whirlpool; laundry/dry cleaning. *In room:* A/C, TV, dataport, iron.

Candy Cane Inn 🎟🎟 *Value*   Take your standard U-shaped motel court with outdoor corridors, spruce it up with cobblestone drives and walkways, old-time street lamps, and flowering vines engulfing the balconies of attractively painted rooms, and you have the Candy Cane. The facelift worked, making this gem near Disney's main gate a treat for the stylish bargain hunter. The guest rooms are decorated in bright floral motifs with comfortable furnishings, including queen beds and a separate dressing and vanity area. Breakfast is served in the courtyard, where you can also splash around in a heated pool, whirlpool, or kids' wading pool.

1747 S. Harbor Blvd., Anaheim, CA 92802. (© 800/345-7057 or 714/774-5284. Fax 714/772-5462. 173 units. $84–$129 double. Rates include expanded continental breakfast. AAA discount available. AE, DC, DISC, MC, V. Free parking and Disney shuttle. **Amenities:** Outdoor pool; whirlpool; wading pool; laundry/dry cleaning; coin-op laundry. *In room:* A/C, TV, coffeemaker, hair dryer.

Howard Johnson Hotel 🎟 *Value*   This hotel occupies an enviable location, directly opposite Disneyland, and a cute San Francisco trolley car runs to and from the park entrance every 30 minutes. Guest rooms were renovated in 1999. They're divided among several low-profile buildings, all with balconies opening onto a central garden with two heated pools. Garden paths lead under eucalyptus and olive trees to a splashing circular fountain. During the summer you can see the nightly fireworks display at Disneyland from the upper balconies of the park-side rooms. Try to avoid the rooms in the back buildings, which get some freeway noise. Services and facilities include room service from the attached coffee shop/diner, airport shuttle, and family lodging/Disney admission packages. We think it's pretty classy for a HoJo's.

1380 S. Harbor Blvd., Anaheim, CA 92802. (© 800/422-4228 or 714/776-6120. Fax 714/533-3578. www.hojoanaheim.com. 320 units. $74–$109 double. AE, DC, DISC, MC, V. Free parking and Disney trolley. **Amenities:** Restaurant; 2 outdoor pools; whirlpool; concierge; game room; room service (7am to 11pm); laundry/dry cleaning; coin-op laundry. *In room:* A/C, TV w/pay movies, dataport, fridge, coffeemaker.

Value **Super-Cheap Sleeps**

When you simply must shave a few *more* dollars off the hotel tariff, try these bargain-priced chains within easy reach of Disneyland: **Anaheim at the Park Travelodge**, 1166 W. Katella Ave (*©* **800/578-7878** or 714/774-7817), which makes up for being a long walk from the park (no shuttle) by offering regular rates of only $51–$89—AAA members and seniors can stay as low as $44. This basic chain motel does, however, boast a nice swimming pool with separate whirlpool, kids' pool, and small playground; or **Super 8 Motel Disneyland Park,** 415 W. Katella Ave. (*©* **800/800-8000** or 714/778-6900), a large impersonal budget property one block from the park. It's clean, basic, and functional, but little extras like a Disneyland shuttle and heated swimming pool help—so do the nice low room rates of $44–$59 (AAA and senior discounts available).

ELSEWHERE IN ORANGE COUNTY
VERY EXPENSIVE

Portofino Beach Hotel *☞*   This oceanfront inn, built in a former seaside rail station, is located just steps away from the Newport Pier, along a stretch of beachy bars and equipment-rental shacks; the beach is across the parking lot. The place maintains a calm, European air even in the face of the midsummer beach frenzy. Although it can get noisy in summer, there are advantages to being at the center of the action. The hotel has its own enclosed parking, and sunsets are spectacular when viewed from a plush armchair in the upstairs parlor. Guest rooms, furnished with old-world antique reproductions, are on the second floor—the first is occupied by a guests-only bar and several cozy sitting rooms—and most have luxurious skylit bathrooms. Though only about 20 minutes away from Disneyland, the Newport seaside is a world away in ambiance (and a dozen degrees cooler in summer).

2306 W. Ocean Front, Newport Beach, CA 92663. *©* **949/673-7030.** Fax 949/723-4370. www.portofinobeachhotel.com. 20 units. $159–$279 double. Rates include continental breakfast. Free parking. AE, DC, DISC, MC, V. **Amenities:** Whirlpool; dry-cleaning/laundry; coin-op laundry. *In room:* A/C, TV.

Westin South Coast Plaza *☞☞*   This sleek and chic upscale business hotel adjacent to the mammoth South Coast Plaza shopping mall is a sure bet for a good night's sleep. Touted as "ten layers of heaven"—from custom pillowtop mattress to the down comforter and family of pillows—Westin offers the best bed in the business. Disneyland is 15 minutes away via the Disney shuttle that stops nearby, and serious shopping is also close, with the state's largest (and finest) mall complex next door—South Coast Plaza is a tourist attraction all by itself. Westin courts business travelers with their "Guest Office" rooms, which feature laser printer/fax and a work area with speakerphone—families will appreciate the Westin Kids Club, which goes beyond day care with amenities like safety kits, jogging strollers, cribs, and souvenir cups or sports bottles.

686 Anton Blvd., Costa Mesa, CA 92626. ℃ **888/625-5144** or 714/540-2500. Fax 714/662-6695. www.westin.com. 329 units. $189–$299 double; from $349 suite. Discounts and Internet specials available. AE, DC, DISC, MC, V. Free self parking, charge for valet. **Amenities:** Restaurant; lounge; heated outdoor pool; whirlpool; lighted tennis courts; fitness center; full service spa; concierge; free airport shuttle; business center; room service (24 hours); dry cleaning/laundry. *In room:* A/C, TV w/pay movies, dataport, minibar, coffeemaker, hair dryer, iron.

EXPENSIVE

Holiday Inn Hotel and Conference Center 🐸   Situated near

Knott's Berry Farm (but within shuttle reach of the Disney parks), this sprawling Holiday Inn received a complete makeover in 1999, and emerged as a respectable player in the local business hotel scene. With extensive conference facilities, the hotel primarily attracts business travelers; this can often mean nice discounts for leisure travelers, who get to enjoy the elevated level of service practiced for corporate clients—plus all the family-friendly policies Holiday Inns are known for. Rooms all feature attractive and practical white-on-white ceramic bathrooms, along with standard-but-new furnishings that do the trick, especially with room rates that reflect the Holiday Inn's un-trendy out-of-park location.

7000 Beach Blvd., Buena Park, CA 90620. ℃ **800/465-4329** or 714/522-7000. Fax 714/522-3230. 246 units. $100–$159 double. Ask about midweek discounts, breakfast packages, and "Great Rates." Kids 18 and under free in parents' room; kids 12 and under eat free at restaurant. AE, DC, DISC, MC, V. Free parking. **Amenities:** Restaurant; lounge; 2 outdoor heated pools (including wading pool); whirlpool; exercise room; concierge; car rental desk; free area shuttle; business center; room service (6am to 11pm), laundry/dry cleaning; self-service laundromat; executive level rooms (includes breakfast). *In room:* A/C, TV w/pay movies, dataport, coffeemaker, hair dryer, iron.

Radisson Resort Knott's Berry Farm 🐸🐸 *Kids*   Within easy

walking distance of Knott's Berry Farm, this spit-shined Radisson (the former Buena Park Hotel) also offers a free shuttle to Disneyland, 7 miles away. The pristine lobby has the look of a business-oriented hotel, and that it is. But vacationers can also benefit from the elevated level of service. Be sure to ask about "Super Saver" rates (as low as $99—with breakfast—at press time), plus Knott's and Disneyland package deals. The rooms in the nine-story tower were tastefully redecorated when Radisson took over. Doting parents can even treat their kids to a Snoopy-themed room!

7675 Crescent Ave. (at Grand), Buena Park, CA 90620. ✆ 800/333-3333 or 714/995-1111. Fax 714/828-8590. www.radisson.com/buenaparkca. 320 units. $129–$139 double; $159–$299 suite. Discounts and packages available. AE, DC, DISC, MC, V. Free parking and Disneyland shuttle. **Amenities:** 2 restaurants; lounge; outdoor pool; lighted tennis courts; fitness center; whirlpool; video arcade; concierge; 24-hour room service; laundry/dry cleaning; self-service laundry. *In room:* A/C, TV w/pay movies, fax, dataport, coffeemaker, hair dryer, iron, bathrobes, safe.

MODERATE

Newport Channel Inn *Value*   Completely renovated in 1999, this humble hotel makes the most of an enviable location amidst pricey Newport Beach. Perched harborside, rooms offer a glimpse of the yachts cruising in and out of Newport Harbor; the decor is motel-plain, but with the beach just a short walk away (including a scenic sand-side jogging/bike path), it's unlikely you'll spend much time indoors. There's no swimming pool here, but the hotel has a sundeck and offers beach towels for a day in the sand and surf. You'll find Disney freeway close (about 15-20 minutes), but the sea breezes and marina views offer a refreshing contrast to landlocked Anaheim.

6030 W. Coast Hwy., Newport Beach, CA 92663. ✆ 800/255-8614 or 949/642-3030. Fax 949/650-2666. www.newportchannelinn.com. 30 units. $59–$119 double. Packages, senior discounts available. AE, DC, DISC, MC, V. Free parking. **Amenities:** Tennis courts nearby; bike/skate rental nearby; coin-op laundry nearby. *In room:* TV, dataport, coffeemaker, hair dryer, iron.

2 In Los Angeles

L.A.'S WESTSIDE & THE BEACHES
EXPENSIVE

Loews Santa Monica Beach Hotel *Kids*   L.A.'s finest family-friendly hotel also makes a great choice for anybody looking for comfortable accommodations, an A-1 Santa Monica location, outstanding service, and a wealth of first-rate facilities. Loews isn't exactly beachfront; it's on a hill less than a block away, but the unobstructed ocean views are fabulous. The hotel just emerged from a $15 million renovation that erased its greatest disadvantage—dour rooms that didn't live up to the luxury price tag or unparalleled facilities. Those who've been here before will notice the differences immediately upon entering the dramatic atrium lobby, whose nondescript fittings have been replaced with a playful SoCal style that puts greater emphasis on the spectacular ocean views. The formerly dowdy guest rooms have been nicely redone in an inviting, clean-lined contemporary style in light, earthy colors. But the best news is still the fabulous facilities, which include an excellent heated pool, plus the famous-in-its-own-right Pritikin Longevity Center and Spa, with a state-of-the-art gym, yoga and Pilates classes, health and fitness counseling, and full slate of spa and salon services.

1700 Ocean Ave. (south of Colorado Blvd.), Santa Monica, CA 90401. ℂ **800/22-LOEWS** or 310/458-6700. Fax 310/458-6761. www.loewshotels.com. 340 units. $305–$460 double; from $675 suite. Ask about corporate rates, Internet offers, and other discounts. Children under 18 stay free in parent's room. AE, DC, DISC, MC, V. Valet parking $18. Pets under 50 lbs. accepted with $500 refundable deposit, plus $5-per-day cleaning fee. **Amenities:** 3 restaurants; outdoor heated pool and whirlpool; large workout room, steam, and sauna; full-service spa; bike and skate rentals; welcome kit for kids under 10; concierge; car-rental desk; business center; salon; 24-hour room service; dry cleaning/laundry. *In room:* Dataport, minibar, CD player, hair dryer, iron.

W Los Angeles Design-savvy traveler hipsters looking for both a cutting-edge style and familiar comforts will enjoy this 15-story, all-suite hotel near UCLA. The former Westwood Marquis underwent a dramatic transformation in 2000 under new owners, W Hotels, the "boutique" hotel brand backed by corporate giant Starwood Hotels (Westin, Sheraton, St. Regis, and other big-name brands). Hidden behind a severe concrete exterior, this oasis-like property had always had advantages: an all-suite configuration, two lush acres of greenery, and eye-catching '60s architectural detailing, newly liberated from its longstanding sheetrock prison. Each large two-room suite features bold, angular furnishings in dark African *wenge* wood, accented with gray carpeting and soft plum textiles. Luxuries include divinely dressed beds, two 27-inch TVs, two CD players, and cordless phones. The bathrooms are spacious but otherwise unremarkable, safe for inviting waffle-weave robes.

Like the all-black-clad staff (which run around with Secret Service-style headsets), the public spaces are dressed to impress. Mojo restaurant serves Latin-inspired cuisine and colorful cocktails to über-stylish industry types, but ends up being more flash than substance. The riotous bar scene that spills into the lobby Thursday through Saturday nights may turn off more subdued folks. The lovely, well-furnished gardenlike pool area has its own outdoor cafe. The excellent full-service spa will even schedule massages in the boldly striped poolside cabanas.

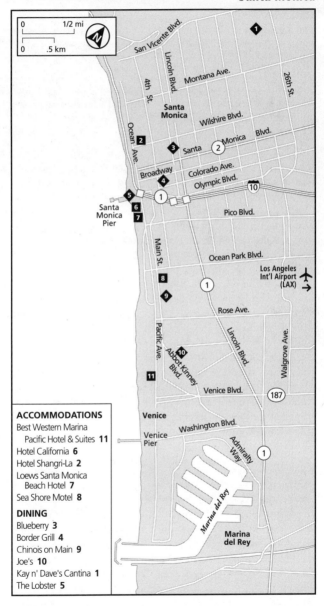

Santa Monica

ACCOMMODATIONS

Best Western Marina
  Pacific Hotel & Suites **11**
Hotel California **6**
Hotel Shangri-La **2**
Loews Santa Monica
  Beach Hotel **7**
Sea Shore Motel **8**

DINING

Blueberry **3**
Border Grill **4**
Chinois on Main **9**
Joe's **10**
Kay n' Dave's Cantina **1**
The Lobster **5**

930 Hilgard Ave., Los Angeles, CA 90024-3033. ℂ 877/W-HOTELS or 310/208-8765. Fax 310/824-0355. 258 units. From $289 1- or 2-bedroom suite. Check for AAA, AARP, and weekend discounts, plus Internet-only rates (usually 10–20% less) and packages ($269 at press time). AE, DC, DISC, MC, V. Valet parking $21. Pets accepted. **Amenities:** Restaurant; cocktail lounge; 2 outdoor heated pools; exercise room; full-service spa; concierge; car-rental desk; courtesy car; business center; 24-hour room service; in-room massage; babysitting; dry cleaning/laundry. *In room:* A/C, TV/VCR with pay movies and Internet access, CD player, dataport, minibar, coffeemaker, hair dryer, iron, laptop-size safe.

MODERATE

Hotel California ℱ *Finds*   New management has remade this former backpackers' flophouse into a clean and welcoming hacienda-style beachfront motel, one that reflects the owner's love of surfing and California beach nostalgia. Boasting an enviable location on Ocean Avenue—right next door to the behemoth Loews—this place embodies the ocean ambience we all want from Santa Monica. The well-tended complex sits above and across an alley from the beach, but it offers excellent views and direct access to the sand via a 5-minute walk along a pretty stepped path. Fully renovated in 2000, the inn offers small but comfortable rooms with brand-new furnishings, including beds with down comforters; freshly refinished woodwork on doors, floors, and decks; retiled bathrooms with all-new fixtures; and lovingly tended landscaping. Five one-bedroom suites also have kitchenettes and pullout sofas that make them great for families or longer stays; all rooms have minifridges and ceiling fans. The suites and some rooms have a partially obstructed ocean view. A handful of rooms have showers only in the bathrooms, so be sure to request a room with a tub from the friendly front-desk staff if it matters to you. *Tip:* Pay a few bucks extra for a courtyard view, as the cheapest rooms face the parking lot and noisy Ocean Avenue.

1670 Ocean Ave. (south of Colorado Ave.), Santa Monica, CA 90401. ℂ 866/571-0000 or 310/393-2363. Fax 310/393-1063. www.hotelca.com. 26 units. $135–$295 double or suite. AE, DISC, MC, V. Self-parking $9. **Amenities:** Whirlpool; activities desk; discount car-rental desk; dry cleaning/laundry; high-speed Internet access, fax/copier, and coffeemaker in front office. *In room:* TV/VCR, dataport, fridge, hair dryer, iron, laptop-size safe.

Hotel Shangri-La   Perched right on Ocean Avenue overlooking the Pacific, in a high-rent residential neighborhood just 2 blocks from Third Street Promenade shopping and dining, the seven-story Shangri-La has a great location. Built in 1939, the hotel sports an ultra-modern exterior and Art Deco interiors to match. The laminated furnishings are downright ugly and the hotel is decidedly low-tech, but considering the location, size, and comfort of these rooms—not to mention the free parking—the Shangri-La is a very good deal. The management is constantly making improvements; on my last visit, the exterior hallways that overlook the large rear courtyard and lead to the rooms had been freshly retiled. Guest rooms, which are mostly studio suites (most with kitchenettes, all with fridges), are spacious, and most offer unencumbered ocean views. Bathrooms are small and simple but clean. The two-bedroom/two-bath suites are a spectacular bargain for large families. Just across the street is a gorgeous stretch of Palisades Park, which overlooks the beach and offers the coast's finest sunset views.

1301 Ocean Ave. (at Arizona Ave.), Santa Monica, CA 90401. © **800/345-STAY** or 310/394-2791. Fax 310/451-3351. www.shangrila-hotel.com. 55 units. $160–$170 studio; from $205 1-bedroom suite, from $330 2-bedroom suite. Rates include continental breakfast and afternoon tea. Inquire about 10% discount for AAA members. AE, DC, DISC, MC, V. Free parking. **Amenities:** Small exercise room; coin-op laundry; dry-cleaning/laundry. *In room:* A/C, TV, dataport, fridge, hair dryer, laptop-size safe.

INEXPENSIVE

Best Western Marina Pacific Hotel & Suites 🐾 *Kids* This bright, newly renovated four-story motel is a haven of smart value just off the rollicking Venice Boardwalk. A simple, contemporary lobby and new elevator lead to spacious rooms brightened with beachy colors and brand-new everything, including chain-standard furnishings, fridges, and two-line phones. The suites are terrific for families; they boast fully outfitted kitchens with microwave and dishwasher, dining areas, pullout sofas, and fireplaces, plus a connecting door that can form a well-priced two-bedroom, two-bath suite. Photos of local scenes and rock-and-roll legends, plus works by local artists, lend the public spaces a wonderful local vibe, and many rooms have at least partial ocean views. Additional incentives include a complimentary coffee-and-Danish continental breakfast, free local shuttle service, and secured parking. Stay elsewhere, though, if you need a lot in the way of service or if you won't relish the party-hearty human carnival of Venice Beach (Santa Monica is generally quieter and more refined). Check both the Best Western reservations line and the direct number for the best rates.

1697 Pacific Ave. (at 17th Ave.), Venice, CA 90291. © **800/780-7234** (Best Western reservations), 800/421-8151 (direct), or 310/452-1111. Fax 310/452-5479. www.mphotel.com or www.bestwestern.com. 88 units. $119–$159 double; $169–$249 suite. Rates include continental breakfast. Extra person $10. Children 12 and under stay free in parents' room. Ask about AAA, senior, and other discounts; weekly and monthly rates also available. AE, DC, DISC, MC, V.

Self-parking $5–$10 (depending on season). **Amenities:** Dry cleaning/laundry; free area shuttle. *In room:* A/C, TV, dataport, fridge, coffeemaker, hair dryer.

Hotel Del Capri *Kids*   This well-located and well-kept Westwood hotel/motel is hugely popular with returning guests, thanks to spacious rooms, a helpful staff, and retro pricing. There are two parts to the Eisenhower-era property: a four-story tower and a charming two-story motel with white louver shutters and delightful flowering vines, whose units surround a pleasant pool. All guest rooms are clean and well cared for, but the decidedly discount decor won't be winning any style awards, and the basic bathrooms could use some upgrading (not to mention quieter fans). Still, every room is comfortable and worth the money; free continental breakfast (delivered to your room) and free parking make a good value even better. The most notable room feature is the electrically adjustable beds, a novel touch; you'll have to request hair dryers and irons if you want them. More than half of the units are one- or two-bedroom suites with kitchenettes, some of which have whirlpool tubs. Nothing is within walking distance of the ritzy high-rise neighborhood, but it's hard to be more freeway-convenient or centrally located. No room service, but nearly 50 restaurants will deliver.

10587 Wilshire Blvd. (at Westholme Ave.), Los Angeles, CA 90024. © **800/ 44-HOTEL** or 310/474-3511. Fax 310/470-9999. www.hoteldelcapri.com. 77 units. $110–$125 double; from $135 suite. Extra person $10. Rates include continental breakfast ($1 gratuity). Price breaks for almost everybody—AAA members, seniors, UCLA grads, military members, and more—so be sure to ask. AE, DC, MC, V. Free parking. **Amenities:** Outdoor pool; tour desk; free area shuttle service with advance notice coin-op laundry; dry cleaning/laundry. *In room:* A/C, TV, adjustable beds.

Sea Shore Motel *Value*   Located in the heart of Santa Monica's best dining and shopping action, this small, friendly, family-run motel is the bargain of the beach. The Sea Shore is such a well-kept secret that most denizens of stylish Main Street are unaware of the incredible accommodations value in their midst. A recent total upgrade of the property—furnishings, fixtures, and exterior—has made the entire place feel fresh and new. Arranged around a parking courtyard, rooms are small and unremarkable; but the conscientious management has done a nice job with them, installing terra-cotta floor tiles, granite countertops, and conveniences like voice mail. Boasting a sitting room and microwave, the suite is a phenomenal deal; book it as far in advance as possible. With a full slate of restaurants out the front door and the Santa Monica Pier and beach just a couple of blocks away, the a terrific bargain base for exploring the sandy side of the city. A deli is attached, selling morning muffins and sandwiches and homemade soup at lunchtime, and a laundromat is next door. A real find!

2637 Main St. (south of Ocean Park Blvd.), Santa Monica, CA 90405. ℂ 310/392-2787. Fax 310/392-5167. www.seashoremotel.com. 20 units. $75–$95 double; $100–$120 suite. Extra person $5. Midweek discounts available. Children under 12 stay free in parents' room. AE, DISC, MC, V. Free parking. Pets accepted for $10-per-night fee. **Amenities:** Deli; coin-op laundry. *In room:* TV, dataport, fridge.

BEVERLY HILLS & HOLLYWOOD
EXPENSIVE

Hyatt West Hollywood   An extensive renovation of this legendary 13-story Sunset Strip hotel erased the last remnants of its former debauched life as the rock 'n' roll "Riot Hyatt." It doesn't even look like other Hyatts, since the management eschewed the corporate decor and contracted locally; the end result is a stylish cross between the clean black-and-white geometrics of a 1930s movie set and a Scandinavian birch-and-ebony aesthetic. While not as fancy as the Mondrian across the street, neither is it as expensive or snobbish. Rooms have city or hillside views (about half have balconies), but stay away from front-facing rooms on the lower floors—too close to noisy Sunset Boulevard. Beyond the smart decor, the standard rooms bear generic but just-fine comforts. Some rooms have coffeemakers (in the works for all rooms at press time), and fridges are available upon request. Suites have VCRs, CD players, wet bars, and fridges, plus a groovy tropical aquarium built into the wall stocked with colorful temporary pets that make the suites worth the extra bucks all by themselves. The rooftop pool is a real plus, offering cushy lounge chairs and a killer perch for peeping into the luxury homes that dot the hill behind the hotel; other brand-new features include a well-equipped exercise room and a new Italian bistro and bar.

8401 Sunset Blvd. (at Kings Rd., 2 blocks east of La Cienega Blvd.), West Hollywood, CA 90069. ℂ 800/233-1234 or 323/656-1234. Fax 323/650-7024. 262 units. $210–$240 double; from $325 suite. Check for discounted weekend, AAA, and senior rates (as low as $155 at press time). Extra person $25; children stay free in parents' room. AE, DC, DISC, MC, V. Valet parking $20; self-parking $10–$15. **Amenities:** Restaurant; bar; coffee/pastry kiosk in lobby; rooftop heated pool; state-of-the-art exercise room; concierge; business center; room service (from 6am to midnight); dry cleaning/laundry; executive-level rooms. *In room:* A/C, TV with pay movies, dataport, hair dryer, iron, safe.

Le Montrose Suite Hotel 🅡 *Value*   Nobody pays rack at this terrific all-suite hotel, which offers money-saving specials of every stripe for travelers who want more than a standard room for their accommodations dollars. Nestled on a quiet residential street 2 blocks from the Sunset Strip, remarkably cozy Le Montrose features large split-level studio and one-bedroom apartments that feel more like comfortable, upscale condos than hotel rooms. Each contemporary-styled suite has a sizable living room with gas fireplace, a dining area, a sleeping nook (or dedicated bedroom), and a nice bathroom. Executive and one-bedroom suites have unstocked kitchenettes (better suited to takeout than actually cooking). The two-bedroom suites are a great deal for families or sharing friends. Tech-friendly goodies abound, including multi-line phones, high-speed connections for your own laptop as well as on-TV Internet access, CD and DVD players, and Nintendo. You have to go up to the roof for anything resembling a view, but once you're up there, you can swim in the pool, soak in the whirlpool, or brush up on your tennis game. This place is a favorite for long-term stays among the music and TV crowd, so don't be surprised if you spot a famous face in the pleasant Library restaurant during the breakfast hour. A $4 million renovation, spiffing up the already very nice digs, should be complete by the time you arrive.

900 Hammond St., West Hollywood, CA 90069. ℭ **800/776-0666** or 310/855-1115. Fax 310/657-9192. www.lemontrose.com. 132 units. $295–$575 suite. Money-saving deals abound; AAA, AARP, seasonal, and weekend rates as low as $159 at press time; breakfast, car, and Disneyland and Universal Studios–inclusive packages also available (from $199). AE, DC, DISC, MC, V. Valet and self-parking $18 Pets accepted with a $100-per-pet nonrefundable fee. **Amenities:** Restaurant; outdoor heated pool with whirlpool and sundeck; lighted tennis court; exercise room with sauna; complimentary bicycles; concierge; Budget car-rental desk; business center; secretarial services; 24-hour room service; coin-op laundry; dry cleaning/laundry; executive-level rooms. *In room:* A/C, TV/VCR with pay movies, Nintendo, Internet access, DVD and CD player, fax/copier/scanner, dataport and high-speed connectivity, minibar, coffeemaker, hair dryer, iron, safe.

MODERATE

Beverly Crescent Hotel   This charming little hotel, the only left coast outpost of New York's Boutique Hotel Group, couldn't be better located: It's on a street a block from Rodeo Drive shopping, but a world away from Golden Triangle congestion. Built in 1926 as a day sleeper for silent-movie stars, the two-story walk-up has been renovated in a pastel-hued, country-in-the-city style. Management and staff are conscientious and professional, and the whole property is impeccably maintained. The bright, pretty guest rooms are outfitted with wood and rattan furniture, and down-filled duvets on the brand-new beds. Other niceties include a work desk,

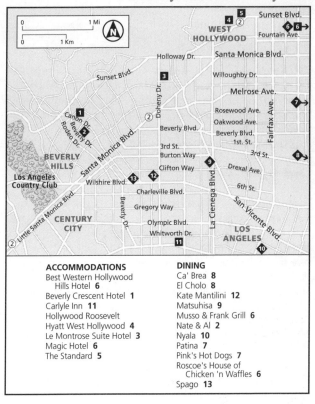

Beverly Hills & West Hollywood

ACCOMMODATIONS
Best Western Hollywood
Hills Hotel **6**
Beverly Crescent Hotel **1**
Carlyle Inn **11**
Hollywood Roosevelt
Hyatt West Hollywood **4**
Le Montrose Suite Hotel **3**
Magic Hotel **6**
The Standard **5**

DINING
Ca' Brea **8**
El Cholo **8**
Kate Mantilini **12**
Matsuhisa **9**
Musso & Frank Grill **6**
Nate & Al **2**
Nyala **10**
Patina **7**
Pink's Hot Dogs **7**
Roscoe's House of
Chicken 'n Waffles **6**
Spago **13**

waffle-weave robes, free bottled water, and free continental breakfast and all-day snacks, which you can enjoy on the gardenlike furnished brick terrace.

So what's the catch? The standard rooms with one double bed are pitifully small, and most have a wall rack with shelves for storage, rather than a real closet. The double/doubles and queen superiors are more spacious, while the king rooms are downright large and come with CD players. Some baths could use a bit of modernizing, but all are spotlessly kept. The Beverly Crescent is best for folks who prize location and an intimate, personalized atmosphere above all else; if you need your space, stick with a king or stay elsewhere. Rack rates are too high, but management will deal—so ask for discounts.

403 N Crescent Dr. (at Brighton Way), Beverly Hills, CA 90210. ☎ **877/847-4444** or 310/247-0505. Fax 310/247-9053. www.beverlycrescenthotel.com. 38 units.

$159–$249 double. Rates include continental breakfast and afternoon tea and cookies. Check for Internet specials (as low as $119 at press time). AE, DC, DISC, MC, V. Parking $12. **Amenities:** Dry cleaning/laundry. *In room:* A/C, TV, dataport, hair dryer, free bottled water.

Carlyle Inn ☆☆ *Value*   Tucked away on an uneventful stretch of Robertson Boulevard just south of Beverly Hills, this four-story inn is one of L.A.'s best mid-priced finds. Making the most of a small lot, architects have created an attractive interior courtyard, which almost every room faces, that gives the property a feeling of openness and serenity that most others in this price range lack—not to mention good outdoor space for enjoying the free breakfast or afternoon munchies at umbrella-covered cafe tables on nice days. The well-planned, contemporary guest rooms are fitted with recessed lighting, Art Deco-inspired furnishings, new firm bedding, well-framed architectural monoprints, plus extras like VCRs and bathrobes. Suites have a pullout sofa but are only slightly larger than standard rooms, so families may be better off in a double/double or connecting rooms. The conscientious manager keeps everything in racing form. The hotel's primary drawback is that it lacks views; curtains must remain drawn at all times to maintain any sense of privacy. Still, it doesn't seem to bother the 90% repeat clientele, who know good value when they find it.

1119 S. Robertson Blvd. (between Pico and Olympic blvds.), Los Angeles, CA 90035. ℂ 800/322-7595 or 310/275-4445. Fax 310/859-0496. www.carlyle-inn.com. 32 units. $120–$209 double; from $140 suite. Rates include buffet breakfast and weekday afternoon hors d'oeuvres. Ask for discounts. AE, DC, DISC, MC, V. Parking $10. **Amenities:** Whirlpool; sundeck; exercise room; dry cleaning/laundry. *In room:* A/C, TV/VCR, minibar, coffeemaker, iron, safe.

Hollywood Roosevelt ☆ *Kids*   This 12-story movie-city landmark is located on a touristy but no longer seedy section of Hollywood Boulevard, across from Mann's Chinese Theatre and just down the street from the Walk of Fame. This Tinseltown legend—host to the first Academy Awards, not to mention a few famousname ghosts—is a great value, since you get an A-1 location and buckets of Hollywood history, plus comforts and services that usually cost twice the price. The rooms are typical of chain hotels, and less appealing than the exquisitely restored public areas; still, they're comfortable, and double/doubles suit small families just fine. Those on the upper floors have unbeatable skyline views, while cabana rooms have a balcony or patio overlooking the Olympic-size pool, whose mural was painted by David Hockney, and poolside bar. The specialty suites are named after stars that stayed in them during the glory days; some have grand verandas. The Cinegrill supper club draws locals with live jazz and top-notch cabaret entertainment.

7000 Hollywood Blvd., Hollywood, CA 90028. (C) **800/950-7667** or 323/466-7000. Fax 323/462-8056. www.hollywoodroosevelt.com. 330 units. $149–$219 double; from $239 suite. Ask about AAA, senior, business, government, and other discounted rates (as low as $89 at press time). Children under 18 stay free. AE, DC, DISC, MC, V. Valet parking $12. **Amenities:** Restaurant; cocktail lounge; nightclub; coffee bar; poolside bar; outdoor pool and whirlpool; exercise room; concierge; activities desk; car-rental desk; business center; room service (6am–11pm); babysitting; dry cleaning/laundry; executive-level rooms. *In room:* A/C; TV with pay movies, video games, and on-screen Internet access, dataport, minibar, coffeemaker, hair dryer, iron; laptop-size safe.

The Standard 🗶🗶 If Andy Warhol had gone into the hotel business (which he no doubt would have, if he had arrived on the scene a few decades later), the Standard would've been the end result. Designed to appeal to the under-35 hipsters, Andre Balazs's West Hollywood neo-motel is sometimes silly, sometimes brilliant, and always provocative (and crowded!). It's a scene worthy of its Sunset Strip location: Shag carpeting on the lobby ceiling, blue astroturf around the swimming pool, a DJ spinning ambient sounds while a performance artist showing more skin than talent poses in a display case behind the check-in desk—this place is definitely left of center.

The good news is that that Standard is more than just a pretty (wild) face. Constructed from the fine bones of a vintage 1962 motel, it boasts comfortably sized rooms outfitted with cobalt-blue indoor-outdoor carpeting, silver beanbag chairs, safety-orange tiles in the bathrooms, and Warhol's Poppy-print curtains, plus private balconies, cordless phones, VCRs, CD players, and minibars whose contents include goodies like sake, condoms, and animal crackers. Look past the retro clutter and often-raucous party scene, and you'll find a level of service more often associated with hotels costing twice as much. On the downside, the cheapest rooms face noisy Sunset Boulevard, no rooms are set aside for non-smokers, and the relentless scene can get tiring if you're not into it.

8300 Sunset Blvd. (at Sweetzer Ave.), West Hollywood, CA 90069. (C) **323/650-9090.** Fax 323/650-2820. www.standardhotel.com. 140 units. $95–$225 double; from $650 suite. AE, DC, DISC, MC, V. Valet parking $18. Pets under 30 lbs. accepted for $100-per-pet fee. **Amenities:** 24-hour coffee shop; poolside cafe; bar/lounge; outdoor heated pool; access to nearby health club; concierge; barbershop; 24-hour room service; in-room massage; dry cleaning/laundry. *In room:* A/C, TV/VCR with pay movies, CD player, dataport and high-speed connection, minibar.

INEXPENSIVE

Best Western Hollywood Hills Hotel 𝒦 Location is a big selling point for this family-owned (since 1948) member of the reliable
Best Western chain: It's just off U.S. 101 (the Hollywood Freeway),
a Metro Line stop just 3 blocks away means easy car-free access to
Universal Studios, and the famed Hollywood and Vine intersection
is just a walk away. The walls showcase images from the golden age
of movies, and the front desk offers an endless variety of arranged
tours. Rooms are plain and clean but lack warmth—outer walls are
painted cinder block, and closets are hidden behind metal accordion
doors. Still, management is constantly striving to improve the hotel,
and all rooms have a refrigerator, a coffeemaker, a microwave, and
free movies. Rooms in the back building are my favorites, as they sit
well back from busy Franklin Avenue, face the gleaming blue-tiled,
heated outdoor pool, and have an attractive view of the neighboring
hillside. The newish bathrooms are jazzier in the front building,
though.

6141 Franklin Ave. (between Vine and Gower sts.), Hollywood, CA 90028. © 800/
287-1700 in CA only, or 323/464-5181. Fax 323/962-0536. www.bestwestern.com/
hollywoodhillshotel. 82 units. $79–$129 double. AAA and AARP discounts available. AE, DISC, MC, V. Free covered parking. Small pets accepted with $25-per-night
fee. **Amenities:** Coffee shop; heated outdoor pool; access to nearby health club;
tour desk; coin-op laundry. *In room:* A/C, TV, fridge, coffeemaker, microwave, hair
dryer, iron.

Magic Hotel 𝒦 *(Kids)* *(Value)* Located a stone's throw from
Hollywood Boulevard's attractions, this garden-style hotel/motel at
the base of the Hollywood Hills offers L.A.'s best cheap sleeps. You
won't see the Magic Hotel in a shelter mag spread anytime soon—
the rooms are done in high Levitz style—but the units are spacious,
comfortable, and well kept. Named for the Magic Castle, the landmark illusionist club just uphill, the hotel was once an apartment
building; it still feels nicely private and insulated from Franklin
Avenue's constant stream of traffic. The units are situated around
a pretty swimming-pool courtyard. Most are full, extra-large apartments, with kitchens with microwave and coffeemaker. Several units
also have balconies overlooking the large heated pool. Ideal for
wallet-watching families or long-term stays.

7025 Franklin Ave. (between La Brea and Highland), Hollywood, CA 90028. © 800/
741-4915 or 323/851-0800. Fax 323/851-4926. www.magichotel.com. 49 units.
$79 double; $99–$179 suite. Extra person $10. Off-season and other discounts
available. AE, DC, DISC, MC, V. Free secured parking. **Amenities:** Outdoor pool;
coin-op laundry. *In room:* A/C, TV, dataport coffeemaker, hair dryer, iron, safe.

NEAR UNIVERSAL STUDIOS
EXPENSIVE

Hilton Universal City & Towers   Although this shiny 24-story hotel sits right outside Universal Studios, there's more of a conservative–business-traveler feel here than the raucous family-with-young-children vibe you might expect. Still, free tram service to the theme park and adjacent Universal CityWalk for shopping and dining means that it's hard for families to be better situated. The polished brass and upscale attitude set the business-like tone, and a light-filled glass lobby leads to a seemingly endless series of conference and banquet rooms, the hotel's bread and butter. The oversized guest rooms are tastefully decorated and constantly refurbished, and have exceptional views (even if the modern, mirror-surfaced windows don't actually open). I prefer the adjacent Sheraton (below) for leisure stays, but go for the best rate.

555 Universal Terrace Pkwy., Universal City, CA 91608. © **800/HILTONS** or 818/506-2500. Fax 818/509-2031. www.universalcity.hilton.com. 483 units. $225–$260 double; from $350 suite. Weekend and other discounts often available. AE, DC, DISC, MC, V. Valet parking $16; self-parking $11. **Amenities:** Restaurant; outdoor heated pool and whirlpool; exercise room; concierge; activities desk; car-rental desk; business center; 24-hour room service; babysitting; dry cleaning/laundry service; executive-level rooms. *In room:* A/C, TV with pay movies and video games, dataport, minibar, coffeemaker, hair dryer, iron, safe.

MODERATE

Beverly Garland's Holiday Inn *Kids*   The "Beverly Garland" in this 258-room hotel's name is the actress who played Fred MacMurray's wife on the later Technicolor episodes of *My Three Sons*. Grassy areas and greenery abound at this North Hollywood Holiday Inn, a virtual oasis in the concrete jungle that is most of L.A. The mission-influenced buildings are a bit dated, but if you grew up with *Brady Bunch* reruns, this adds to the charm—the spread looks like something Mike Brady would have designed. Southwestern-themed fabrics complement the natural-pine furnishings in the spacious and recently renovated guest rooms, attracting your attention away from the painted cinder-block walls. On the upside, all of the well-outfitted rooms have balconies overlooking the grounds, and a pool and two lighted tennis courts are on hand. With Universal Studios just down the street and a free shuttle to the park, the location can't be beat for families. Since proximity to the 101 and 134 freeways also means the constant buzz of traffic, ask for a room facing Vineland Avenue for maximum quiet.

4222 Vineland Ave., North Hollywood, CA 91602. © **800/BEVERLY**, 800/HOLIDAY, or 818/980-8000. Fax 818/766-5230. www.beverlygarland.com or www.holiday-inn.com. 267 units. $149–$179 double; from $209 suite. Ask about AAA, AARP, corporate, military, Great Rates, weekend, and other discounted rates (from $109 at press time). Kids 12 and under stay and eat free. AE, DC, DISC, MC, V. Free parking. **Amenities:** Restaurant; heated outdoor pool; lighted tennis courts; sauna; car-rental desk; complimentary shuttle to Universal Studios. *In room:* A/C, TV, coffeemaker, hair dryer, iron.

Radisson Valley Center If you're happy with an affordable, convention-style chain hotel, this may be the choice for you. The Radisson is located at the crossroads of two major freeways, the San Diego (I-405) and Ventura (U.S. 101). Universal Studios, NBC Studios, Magic Mountain, Griffith Park, Hollywood, and Beverly Hills are all just a short freeway ride away. The spacious, attractive rooms have private balconies, two-line phones, and a work desk; the bathrooms and furnishings are just beginning to show their age, but 42 new suites are large (550 square feet) and spanking new. Refrigerators, coffeemakers, and cribs are available upon request. *Money-saving tip:* Ask for discount coupons to Universal Studios at the front desk.

15433 Ventura Blvd., Sherman Oaks, CA 91403. © **800/333-3333** or 818/981-5400. Fax 818/981-3175. www.radisson.com/shermanoaksca. 178 units. $119–$195 double; from $179 suite. Special discount packages available. AE, DC, DISC, MC, V. Self-parking $5.50. **Amenities:** Cafe; cocktail lounge; outdoor heated pool and whirlpool; exercise room; concierge; tour desk; car-rental desk; salon; room service (7am–10pm); coin-op laundry; dry cleaning/laundry; executive-level rooms. *In room:* A/C, TV with pay movies, dataport, coffeemaker, hair dryer, iron.

Sheraton Universal Hotel ⋒ *(Kids)* Despite the addition of the sleekly modern Hilton just uphill, the 21-story Sheraton is still considered "the" Universal City hotel of choice for tourists, businesspeople, and industry folks visiting the studios' production offices. It has a spacious 1960s feel, with updated styling and amenities; although the Sheraton does its share of convention/event business, the hotel feels more leisure-oriented than the Hilton next door (an outdoor elevator connects the two properties). Choose a lanai room for balconies that overlook the lushly planted pool area, or a Tower room for views and solitude. The hotel is very close to the Hollywood Bowl, and you can practically roll out of bed and into the theme park (via a continuous shuttle). An extra $35 per night buys a Club Level room—worth the money for the extra in-room amenities, plus free continental breakfast and afternoon hors d'oeuvres; business rooms also feature a moveable workstation and a fax/copier/printer.

333 Universal Terrace Pkwy., Universal City, CA 91608. © 800/325-3535 or 818/980-1212. Fax 818/985-4980. www.sheraton.com. 442 units. $149–$219 double; from $350 suite. Children stay free in parents' room. Ask about AAA, AARP, and corporate discounts; also inquire about packages that include theme-park admission. AE, DC, DISC, MC, V. Valet parking $16; self-parking $11. **Amenities:** Restaurant; lobby piano lounge; outdoor pool and whirlpool; health club; game room; concierge; free shuttle to Universal Studios every 15 minutes; business center; room service (from 6am–midnight); babysitting; dry cleaning/laundry; executive-level rooms. *In room:* A/C, TV with pay movies and video games, dataport, minibar, safe (hair dryer and iron in club-level rooms).

Sportsmen's Lodge It's been a long time since this part of Studio City was wilderness enough to justify the lodge's name. This sprawling motel has been enlarged and upgraded since, but the lovely garden-like grounds still conjure up images of those days. Done in a country-ish style, guest rooms are large and comfortable but not luxurious; all have balconies or patios. L-shaped studio suites, which can sleep a maximum of 5, and new executive king rooms boast two-line phones, a big work desk with a fax machine, a free welcome cocktail, and a coffeemaker and a hair dryer (amenities that should—and usually do—come standard in all categories these days). Those in standard rooms have to request goodies like hair dryers; fridges are also available. You might take advantage of the lovely pool and patio cafe/bar, which will let you forget all about busy Ventura Boulevard just out the front door; don't miss the black and white swans frolicking out back in the koi-filled ponds. The neighborhood is pleasant and offers easy canyon and freeway access to L.A., but those of you heading to Universal Studios can usually hop a free shuttle. *Money-saving tip:* Ask about discount tickets to Universal, which are usually available at the front desk.

12825 Ventura Blvd. (east of Coldwater Canyon), Studio City, CA 91604. © 800/821-8511 or 818/769-4700. Fax 818/769-4798. www.slhotel.com. 191 units. $122–$172 double; from $180 suite. Ask about discounted AAA and AARP rates; Internet specials as low as $99 at press time. AE, DC, DISC, MC, V. Free parking. **Amenities:** Restaurant; bar; outdoor heated Olympic-size pool and whirlpool; exercise room; activities desk; car-rental desk; courtesy shuttle to Burbank Airport and Universal Studios; salon; room service (6:45am–8:45pm); coin-op laundry; dry cleaning/laundry. *In room:* A/C, TV.

INEXPENSIVE

Best Western Mikado Hotel This Asian-flavored garden hotel has been a Valley fixture for 40-plus years. A complete 1999 renovation muted but didn't obliterate the kitsch value, which extends from the pagoda-style exterior to the sushi bar (the Valley's oldest) across the driveway. Two-story motel buildings face two well-maintained courtyards, one with a koi pond and wooden foot-bridge, the other with a shimmering blue-tiled pool and hot tub. The facelift stripped most of the Asian vibe from guest rooms, which are fresh feeling, comfortable, and well outfitted. Furnished in 1970s-era chic (leather sofas, earth tones), the one-bedroom apartment is a steal, with enormous rooms and a full-size kitchen.

12600 Riverside Dr. (between Whitsett and Coldwater Canyon), North Hollywood, CA 91607. (©) **800/826-2759,** 800/433-2239 in CA, or 818/763-9141. Fax 818/752-1045. www.bestwestern.com/mikadohotel. 58 units. $129–$139 double; $175 1-bedroom apartment. Rates include full breakfast. Ask about AAA, senior, and other discounted rates (as low as $98 at press time). Extra person $10. Children under 12 stay free. Rates include full American breakfast. AE, DC, DISC, MC, V. Free parking. **Amenities:** Japanese restaurant and sushi bar, cocktail lounge; outdoor pool and whirlpool; fax and copying services at front desk. *In room:* A/C, TV, dataport, coffeemaker, hair dryer, iron.

Safari Inn (**Finds** This 1957-vintage motel is so deliciously retro that it—and its landmark neon sign—have starred in such films as *Apollo 13* and *True Romance*. The exterior is gloriously intact (note the groovy wrought-iron railings and the floating stone fireplace in the lobby, mid-century buffs), while the interiors have been upgraded with a smart, colorful SoCal look and all the modern comforts. Everything within is 21st-century new, including the attractive IKEA-style furniture, the bright contemporary textiles and wallprints, and the sparkling modern bathrooms; about ten rooms also have microkitchens (basically wet bars) with a microwave. Everything is clean, fresh, and pleasing. Attention families: Book now to snare one of the two in-demand suites, which have pullout sofas, huge closets, full kitchens, and a second TV.

Located just down the street from the movie studios, the neighborhood is modest but quiet and nice, and convenient for those interested in studio tours, TV-show tapings, and easy freeway access to Universal Studios. In classic motor lodge style, a petite pool sits in a gated corner of the parking lot, but it's attractive and inviting on hot Valley days. Other amenities that elevate the Safari above the motel standard include an exercise room sporting all-new equipment, room service from the modest but good restaurant at the Annabelle Hotel (the Safari's sister property) next door, and valet service as well as self-serve laundry.

1911 W Olive Ave., Burbank, CA 91506. (©) **818/845-8586.** Fax 818/845-0054. 55 units. $109–$139 double; $168 suite. AAA and corporate rate $95. Extra person $10. AE, DC, DISC, MC, V. Free parking. Pets accepted with $100 deposit. **Amenities:** Restaurant and martini bar (next door); heated outdoor pool; exercise room; sundeck; limited room service; coin-op laundry; dry cleaning/laundry. *In room:* TV with pay movies, dataport, coffeemaker, fridge, iron, hair dryer.

5

Dining

There's nothing quite like an energetic family vacation to build an appetite, and sooner or later we'll all have to make the important dining decisions: where, when, and how much?

The expanded Disneyland Resort has something for everyone, a respectable lineup that can easily meet your needs for the duration of the typical visit. Until recently, dining options were pretty sparse—limited to those inside Disneyland and some old standbys at the Disneyland Hotel. But Disney's big expansion upped the ante with national theme/concept restaurants along Downtown Disney, and newly competitive dining at the resort hotels. We've included the best of the field in this chapter, as well as several notable choices in surrounding Orange County for those with a hankering to explore. Because Los Angeles is often the base for Disney visitors, you'll also find a broad selection of great choices in L.A.'s most popular neighborhoods.

All our listed restaurants are categorized by price as follows: *Expensive* = over $45 per person (for an appetizer, main course, dessert, and non-alcoholic beverage, at **dinner**); *Moderate* = between $20 and $44; *Inexpensive* = under $19. Some general rules of thumb for keeping your food expenditures down are:

- Remember that even some of the priciest spots are a lot more affordable at lunch; most of our listings include lunch prices for comparison.
- Does your hotel rate include breakfast? If so, take full advantage (perhaps slip a piece of fruit into your pocket for later).
- Does your hotel room have a fridge or kitchenette? Remember this when ordering in restaurants, particularly those with large portions—tonight's leftovers could be tomorrow's lunch.
- Remember to pack some quick pick-me-ups (granola bars, candy, or fresh fruit)—and don't forget a few goodies for the kids, too. That way, your dining budget won't get eaten away (no pun intended) by cotton candy, ice cream bars, and disappointing fast food inside the theme parks.

- *For adults only:* Alcoholic beverages at restaurants and bars will make your costs skyrocket, so keep tabs on your drinks to avoid an unexpected surprise when the bill comes.

For locations of the eateries listed below, see the maps in chapter 4, "Accommodations" and chapter 6, "What to See and Do at the Disneyland Resort."

1 Inside the Theme Parks

One thing's for sure, you'll go broke before you go hungry at the Disneyland Resort. There's food everywhere, from more than a dozen sit-down restaurants and cafeterias inside the two parks to eight at the three Resort hotels and eight more in Downtown Disney (see full listings, below)—and that isn't even counting snack carts, casual walk-up stands, and packaged food shops! Overall, we have to admit that most snack concessions inside Disneyland and California Adventure are overrated, overcrowded, *and* overpriced, redeeming themselves only with the convenience of being at hand whenever and wherever your blood sugar takes a dive. Some noteworthy exceptions can be found in the "Snacking, Disney Style" box, below.

OTHER DINING INSIDE THE PARKS

When you're looking for a sit-down meal during a day of theme-parking, there are many choices. Here's a thumbnail sketch of some other in-park eateries, all of which are family-friendly. Expect prices to be higher than average, reflecting the food-as-entertainment aspect of Disney dining—and also remember that it's easy to hop the monorail or shuttle outside the parks, where you can choose from Downtown Disney's establishments, hotel restaurants, or even an affordable coffee shop across the street.

- Though the food itself is what you'd find in an unremarkable Southern coffee shop, it's hard to resist New Orleans Square's **Blue Bayou Restaurant.** The only eatery inside Disneyland that requires reservations (stop by early in the day to make yours), it meticulously recreates a classic New Orleans verandah, complete with lush, vine-wrapped ironwork, chirping crickets, and (non-alcoholic) mint juleps. Its misty, sunless atmosphere comes from being literally inside the Pirates of the Caribbean ride, so boatloads of pirate-bound riders drift subtly by during your meal!

Tips Snacking, Disney Style

- Scattered throughout Disneyland—but thankfully plotted on the official Park map—are **churro carts,** which dispense these absolutely addictive cylindrical Mexican donuts (rolled in sugar) beginning at 11am.
- If you're beginning to think there are no healthy snack options inside the Park, head to Adventureland for refreshments at the **Tiki Juice Bar** and **Indy Fruit Cart,** which offer tropical juices and unembellished fresh fruit for a natural sugar boost. (Disneyland)
- Anyone with a sweet tooth won't want to miss Main Street's **Candy Kitchen,** purveyor of old-style treats like caramel apples, candy ribbons, and chocolate nonpareils. The exhibition kitchen's enormous copper vats and marble worktables are put to use throughout the day, offering a glimpse into how candy canes are twisted into barber-shop-pole perfection or chocolate fudge gets its velvety texture. (Disneyland)
- Along the Paradise Pier boardwalk (just behind the giant Orange Stinger ride), **Corn Dog Castle** is home to this traditional beach snack; they serve little else, and the freshly deep-fried dogs are big enough for two to share. (California Adventure)
- For an interactive change-of-pace, head to Pacific Wharf for a trio of mouth-watering "attractions" reminiscent of grade-school fieldtrips to name-brand factories. At the demonstration kitchens for Boudin Bakery, Mission Tortillas, and Lucky Fortune Cookies, you can follow up with a traditional snack featuring the products you saw being made: soup in a Boudin sourdough bowl, tacos and burritos on Mission tortillas, or Chinese rice bowls and egg rolls followed by a fresh fortune cookie. (California Adventure)

- The original Disney park hasn't caught up with California Adventure's new generation of stylish in-park eateries; outside of these, the best food and value inside Disneyland is the almost-hidden **Redd Rockett's Pizza Port,** a Buitoni-brand-sponsored cafeteria near the entrance to Space Mountain.

Freshly prepared, towering platters of Italian salads, pastas, and thick-crust pizza taste better than expected, and fill the bill for hungry families.

• When hunger pangs strike inside California Adventure, stagger dramatically into the kitschy **Soap Opera Bistro** on the Hollywood Pictures Backlot. Built of actual sets from ABC daytime dramas like *All My Children* (Chandler's mansion), *General Hospital* (Luke's diner, a nurses' station), and *One Life to Live* (Llanview Country Club), this soap-addict's heaven goes the distance with "auditioning" servers (who occasionally break into performance). The something-for-everyone menu is tailored to the theme (look for "Erica's chicken salad" or "Port Charles Chilean sea bass"), your mealtime will be peppered with backstage information on the serials, and an attached memorabilia shop even sells collectibles from several series.

THE REST OF THE RESORT: DOWNTOWN DISNEY & THE DISNEY HOTELS
EXPENSIVE

Napa Rose ☆☆☆ CALIFORNIA   Situated inside the upscale Grand Californian Hotel, Napa Rose is the first really serious (read: on "foodie" radar) restaurant at the Disneyland Resort. Its warm and light dining room mirrors the Arts and Crafts style of the hotel, down to Frank Lloyd Wright stained-glass windows and Craftsman-inspired seating throughout the restaurant and adjoining lounge. Executive chef Andrew Sutton was lured away from the Napa Valley's chic Auberge du Soleil, bringing with him a wine-country sensibility and passion for fresh California ingredients and inventive

---

Fun Fact **Cocktails with Mickey?**

Disneyland has been known for years as a teetotaler's paradise, a family destination devoid of alcoholic beverages. Not any more . . .

Though you'll certainly not be seeing folks traipsing down Main Street clutching a brown-bagged fifth (in fact, alcohol is still not available in any of the public areas of Disneyland), Downtown Disney features independently operated restaurants and clubs, many of which feature impressively stocked bars, wine cellars, and inventive cocktail menus. Cheers!

---

preparations. You can see him busy in the impressive open exhibition kitchen, showcasing specialty items like Sierra golden trout, artisan cheeses from Humboldt County and the Gold Country, and the Sonoma rabbit in Sutton's signature braised mushroom-rabbit tart. The tantalizing "Seven Sparkling Sins" starter platter (for two) features jewel-like portions of *foie gras,* caviar, oysters, lobster, and other exotic delicacies; the same attention to detail is evident in seasonally composed main course standouts like grilled yellowtail with tangerine-basil fruit salsa atop savory couscous, or free-range veal osso buco in rich bacon-forest mushroom ragout. Leave room for dessert, to at least share one of pastry chef Jorge Sotello's creative treats—our favorites are Sonoma goat cheese flan with Riesling-soaked tropical fruit, and chocolate crêpes with house-made caramelized banana ice cream. Napa Rose boasts an impressive and balanced wine list, with 45 by-the-glass choices; and outdoor seating is arranged around a rustic fire pit, gazing out across a landscaped arroyo toward California Adventure's distinctive Grizzly Peak.

1600 S. Disneyland Dr. (in Disney's Grand Californian Hotel). © 714/300-7170. www.disneyland.com. Reservations strongly recommended. Main courses $12–$16 lunch, $19–$30 dinner. AE, DC, DISC, MC, V. Daily 11:30am–2pm and 5:30–10pm.

Yamabuki ⋘ JAPANESE   Often ignored by all but their thriving clientele of Asian tourists and business folk—plus in-the-know expense account suits from surrounding Orange County—Yamabuki has been tucked away for years in the low-profile former Pacific Hotel (now reinvented as Disney's Paradise Pier Hotel). With an upscale and quietly traditional Japanese aesthetic, Yamabuki—the name of a Japanese rose—has a rich interior of deep red lacquer, delicate porcelain vases, discreet teak shutters, and translucent rice paper screens that together impart a sense of very un-Disney nobility. The staff is elegantly kimono-clad—even at lunch, when the fare includes casual bento boxes, lunch specials, and sushi/sashimi selections. At dinner, tradition demands a languorous procession of courses, from refreshing seafood starters and steaming noodle bowls to grilled teriyaki meats or table-cooked specialties like sukiyaki or *shabu shabu.* The menu, in Japanese and English, rates each dish as "contemporary," "traditional," or "very traditional," presenting the opportunity to try unusual squid, soybean, and pickled root dishes common in the East. If you're willing to spend the time—and the money—Yamabuki is a cultural trip across the globe.

1717 S. Disneyland Dr. (in Disney's Paradise Pier Hotel). ⓒ **714/239-5683**; reservations 714/956-6755. www.disneyland.com. Reservations recommended at dinner. Main courses $7.50–$11 lunch, $14–$30 dinner. AE, DC, DISC, MC, V. Mon–Fri 11:30am–2pm, daily 5:30–10pm.

MODERATE

Catal Restaurant/Uva Bar ⭐⭐ MEDITERRANEAN/TAPAS

Branching out from acclaimed Patina restaurant in Los Angeles, high-priest-of-cuisine Joachim Splichal brings us this Spanish-inspired Mediterranean concept duo at the heart of Downtown Disney. The main restaurant, Catal, features a series of intimate second-floor rooms that combine rustic Mediterranean charm with fine dining. Complemented by an international wine list, the menu is a collage of flavors that borrow from France, Spain, Italy, Greece, Morocco, and the Middle East—all united in selections that manage to be intriguing but not overwhelming. Though the menu will vary seasonally, expect to find selections that range from seared sea scallops over saffron risotto or chorizo-spiked Spanish paella to herb-marinated rotisserie chicken or Sicilian rigatoni with ricotta cheese.

Downstairs, the Uva Bar (*uva* means "grape" in Spanish) is a casual tapas bar offering 40 different wines by the glass in an outdoor pavilion setting. The affordable menu features the same pan-Mediterranean influence, even offering many items from the Catal menu; standouts include cabernet-braised short ribs atop horseradish mashed potatoes, marinated olives and cured Spanish ham, and Andalusian gazpacho with rock shrimp.

1580 Disneyland Dr. (at Downtown Disney). ⓒ **714/774-4442**. Reservations recommended Sun–Thur, not accepted Fri–Sat (Catal); not accepted for Uva Bar. Main courses $14–$24, tapas $5–$8. AE, DC, DISC, MC, V. Mon–Thurs 11am–11pm, Fri–Sun 11am–midnight.

Goofy's Kitchen 🄺🄸🄳🅂 AMERICAN   Your younger kids will never

forgive you if they miss an opportunity to dine with their favorite Disney characters at this colorful, lively restaurant inside the Disneyland Hotel. Known for its entertainment and wacky and off-center Toontown-esque decor, Goofy's Kitchen features tableside visits by costumed Disney characters from the classic era (Snow White, Mickey Mouse) to the new generation (Pocahontas, Buzz Lightyear), who delight the youngsters with mini-performances, autograph signing, and up-close-and-personal encounters. Meals are buffet-style, and offer an adequate selection of crowd pleasers and reliable standbys from bacon and eggs at breakfast to fried chicken,

Caesar salad, deli sandwiches, and Italian pastas at lunch and dinner: this place isn't really about the food, though, and is definitely *not* for kid-less grownups (unless you're trying to make up for a deprived childhood). You'll also want to remember a camera for capturing the family's "candid" encounters.

1150 Magic Way (inside the Disneyland Hotel). © 714/956-6755. www. disneyland. com. Reservations recommended. Buffet prices (child/adult): $10/17 breakfast, $10/18 lunch, $10/27 dinner. AE, DC, DISC, MC, V. Daily 7am–9pm.

House of Blues ⑆ AMERICAN/SOUTHERN

For years fans have been comparing the House of Blues to Disneyland, so this celeb-backed restaurant/nightclub fits right into the Disney compound. Locations in Las Vegas, L.A., Orlando, and so forth all sport a calculated backwoods-bayou-meets-Country-Bear-Jamboree appearance that fits right into the Disneyfied world. The Anaheim HOB follows the formula, filled with made-to-look-old found objects, amateur paintings, uneven wood floors, seemingly decayed chandeliers, and a country-casual attitude. The restaurant features Delta-inspired stick-to-your-ribs cuisine like Louisiana crawfish cakes, Creole seafood jambalaya, cornmeal-crusted catfish, baby back ribs glazed with Jack Daniels sauce, and spicy Cajun meatloaf—plus some out-of-place Cal-lite stragglers like seared ahi and pesto pasta. Sunday's Gospel Brunch is an advance-ticket event of hand-clapping, foot-stomping proportions, and the adjacent Company Store offers logo ware interspersed with selected pieces of folk art. HOB's state-of-the-art Music Hall is a welcome addition to the local music scene (advance tickets are highly recommended for big-name bookings; see chapter 7, "After Dark Entertainment & Nightlife," for more information).

1530 S. Disneyland Dr. (at Downtown Disney). © 714/778-2583. www.hob.com. Reservations not accepted for restaurant (tickets required for performance). Main courses $8–$17. AE, DC, DISC, MC, V. Daily 11am–midnight (open from 10am Sun).

Naples Ristorante e Pizzeria ⑆ ITALIAN

The eye-catching entrance of this better-than-expected Italian concept eatery features a larger-than-life harlequin with an impish expression, wielding a pizza and beckoning you to step inside. Designed to be sophisticated enough for discerning palates while still appropriate for casual families, Naples features a colorful, high-ceilinged dining room filled with padded loveseats and comfy chairs. Busy chefs work the white-tiled open kitchen's wood-burning oven, while a floor-to-ceiling cherry-wood bar anchors the other side of the room. Naples also boasts some of the most scenic outdoor seating in Downtown

Disney—request a patio table when reserving. At dinner, you can also opt for the quieter ambiance of the upstairs dining room. Piedmontese executive chef Corrado Gionatti is a master of the thin-crust Neapolitan pizza, and uses an appropriately light hand saucing the menu's selection of pastas. Salads, antipasti, and calzone round out the menu; everything is very good, and—be forewarned—portions are quite large.

1550 Disneyland Dr. (at Downtown Disney). ✆ **714/776-6200.** Reservations strongly recommended. Main courses $11–$16. AE, DC, DISC, MC, V. Daily 11am–11pm.

Rainforest Cafe *Kids* INTERNATIONAL   Designed to suggest ancient temple ruins in an overgrown Central American jungle, this national chain favorite successfully combines entertainment, retail, and family-friendly dining in one fantasy setting. There are cascading waterfalls inside and out, a canopy of lush vegetation, simulated tropical mists, and even a troupe of colorful parrots beckoning shoppers into the "Retail Village." Once seated, diners choose from an amalgam of wildly flavored dishes inspired by Caribbean, Polynesian, Latin, Asian, and Mediterranean cuisines. Masquerading under exotic-sounding names like "Jungle Safari Soup" (a meaty version of minestrone) and "Mojo Bones" (barbecue pork ribs), the food is really fairly familiar: a translated sampling includes Cobb salad, pita sandwiches, potstickers, shrimp-studded pasta, and charbroiled chicken. Fresh fruit smoothies and tropical specialty cocktails are offered, as well as a best-shared dessert called "Giant Chocolate Volcano." After your meal, you can browse through logo items, environmentally educational toys and games, stuffed jungle animals and puppets, straw safari hats, and other themed souvenirs in the lobby store. There's a children's menu, and the Rainforest Cafe is one of the few Downtown Disney eateries to have full breakfast service.

1515 S. Disneyland Dr. (at Downtown Disney). ✆ **714/772-0413.** www. rainforestcafe.com. Reservations recommended for peak mealtimes. Main courses $9–$21. AE, DC, DISC, MC, V. Sun–Thurs 7am–11pm, Fri–Sat 7am–midnight.

Ralph Brennan's Jazz Kitchen *★* CAJUN-CREOLE   If you always thought Disneyland's New Orleans Square was just like the real thing, wait till you see this authentically southern concept restaurant at Downtown Disney. Ralph Brennan, of the New Orleans food dynasty responsible for NOLA landmarks like Commander's Palace and a trio of Big Easy hotspots, commissioned a handful of New Orleans artists to create the handcrafted furnishings that give the Jazz Kitchen its believable French Quarter ambiance. Lacy wrought-iron grillwork, cascading ferns, and trickling stone fountains enhance three separate dining choices: The upstairs Carnival Club is an elegant dining salon with silk-draped chandeliers and terrace dining that overlooks the "street scene" below; casual Flambeaux is downstairs, where a bead-encrusted grand piano hints at the nightly live jazz that sizzles in this room (see chapter 7, "After Dark Entertainment & Nightlife"); and the Creole Cafe is a quick stop for necessities like muffuletta or beignets. Expect traditional Cajun-Creole fare with heavy-handed seasonings and rich, heart-stopping sauces—now *that's* authentically New Orleans.

1590 S. Disneyland Dr. (at Downtown Disney). © 714/776-5200. www. rbjazzkitchen.com. Reservations strongly recommended. Main courses $16–$25 (Cafe items $4–$8). AE, DC, DISC, MC, V. Daily 11am–3pm and 5–11pm.

INEXPENSIVE TO MODERATE

La Brea Bakery Express & Cafe BAKERY/MEDITERRANEAN
Fresh from the ovens of L.A.'s now-nationally-known artisan bakery, this La Brea Bakery duo occupies a coveted position at the beginning of Downtown Disney, right across from the theme parks' ticket kiosks. Each morning still-groggy early-bird parkgoers stumble from the parking-lot tram and head straight to La Brea's cafeteria-style Express for a caffeinated pick-me-up or a meal to start the day— light breakfast items are served in addition to creator Nancy Silverton's irresistible breads and pastries. The outdoor patio is comfortably outfitted with woven bistro chairs (plus heat lamps for brisk mornings), and provides a relaxing setting before braving the Disney throngs. Throughout the day, folks stop in for a lunch of sandwiches, filled brioche, or herb-laden focaccia—the kids' menu offers less-grown-up choices like grilled cheese and PB&J.

Beginning at lunchtime, the next-door Cafe joins the team with sit-down meals, complete with wine-by-the-glass selections. Sporting an airy, warm-wood gallery-like setting, the small bistro also features a few outdoor tables alongside the Downtown Disney footpath. Entrees feature the Mediterranean flavors popularized at Silverton's (with husband Mark Peel) acclaimed Campanile restaurant, and range from the lighter side (seared salmon or ahi) to a hearty lamb/sirloin/sausage stew atop creamy polenta.

1556 Disneyland Dr. (at Downtown Disney). © 714/490-0233. www.labreabakery. com. Reservations recommended for Cafe. Light fare under $5 (Express), Main courses $10–$20 (Cafe). AE, DISC, MC, V. Daily 8am–11pm (Express), 11am–11pm (Cafe).

Y Arriba Y Arriba PAN-LATIN TAPAS   Following the Latin tradition of *tapas-teatro* (tapas bar and theater), Y Arriba Y Arriba is a high-energy crowd-pleaser from a corporation of Miami restaurateurs with decades of experience in Latin-Cuban dinner clubs. Brimming with bold colors and *Carnival*-esque decor, the restaurant features a multi-level open clublike space; a central stage can be raised and lowered, forming a dance floor for patrons or a platform for in-house dancers, the Y Arriba orchestra, or Latin specialty acts. The menu features a progression of snack-size plates drawn from international Latin cultures: Cuban *lechon* (tangy roasted pork), Columbian *arepas* (corn cakes with spicy chorizo); Ecuadorian *llapingachos* (cheesy potato cakes with peanut sauce), Argentinean *churrasco* (tender skirt steak with *chimichurri*), and Chilean *corvina* (sea bass atop a rich corn-squash stew) are just a few. The intermittent music and dancers can seem a little forced at lunchtime, but in the evening—especially after a few rum-laced South American cocktails—the convivial atmosphere (and frequent big-name entertainers) takes center stage; on Thursdays after 10pm, tables are pushed aside for the full-blown Blue Agave dance club.

1510 S. Disneyland Dr. (at Downtown Disney). ✆ **714/533-8272.** www. yarribayarriba.com. Reservations accepted Mon–Thurs only. Tapas $5–$10. AE, DISC, MC, V. Daily 11am–2am.

2 Elsewhere in Orange County

EXPENSIVE

Roy's of Newport Beach 𝄢𝄢 HAWAIIAN REGIONAL/ PACIFIC RIM   Any foodie who's been to Hawaii in the past decade knows the name of Roy Yamaguchi, father of Hawaiian Regional Cuisine (HRC) and the islands' answer to Wolfgang Puck. Roy's empire expanded to Southern California in 1999, with the opening of this successful dinner-only restaurant on the fringe of Fashion Island shopping center. Yamaguchi developed a menu that represents his groundbreaking East/West/Polynesian cuisine but can be reliably executed by chefs in far-flung kitchens. Most of each night's specials are fresh Pacific fish, given the patented HRC touch with Japanese, Thai, and even Latin accents. Signature dishes include island-style ahi poke, spicy Mongolian-glazed rack of lamb, and blackened yellowfin tuna in soy-mustard-butter sauce. The bar whips up "vacation" cocktails in tropical colors, and there's a to-die-for chocolate soufflé dessert.

453 Newport Center Dr., Fashion Island. ✆ **949/640-ROYS.** Reservations suggested. Main courses $16–$29. AE, DC, DISC, MC, V. Mon–Thurs 5–10pm; Fri–Sat 5–11pm.

The White House ✿ ITALIAN & FRENCH   Once surrounded by orange groves, this stately 1909 Colonial-style mansion now sits on a wide industrial street just 5 minutes from Disneyland. It's set nicely back, though, framed by lovely lawns and gardens, and exudes gentility and nostalgia. The huge home is nicely restored inside and out; the restaurant opened in 1981, when it was named after its stylistic cousin in Washington—*the* White House. Owner Bruno Serato maintains this architectural treasure, serving northern Italian cuisine—with a French accent—in elegant white-on-white rooms on the main and second floors. Dinner courses are named for fashion giants (Versace whitefish, Prada rack of lamb), and sometimes arrive on oddly-shaped platters that work better as artwork than dishware. But chef David Libby knows what he's doing, applying just the right amount of sauce to pastas both formal (gnocchi in velvety Gorgonzola sauce) and rustic (linguini with chunky garlic, roasted peppers, and olives). Prices tend to reflect the suited-expense-account and well-heeled-retiree crowd, but lunch prices (including a terrific prix fixe bargain) deliver the same bang for fewer bucks.

887 Anaheim Blvd. (north of Ball Rd.), Anaheim. ✆ **714/772-1381.** www. anaheimwhitehouse.com. Reservations recommended at dinner. Main courses $10–$16 lunch, $18–$28 dinner. AE, MC, V. Mon–Fri 11:30am–2pm and 5–10pm, Sat–Sun 5–10pm.

MODERATE

Citrus City Grille ✿✿ CALIFORNIAN   Though housed in Orange's second-oldest brick building, this sophisticated crowd-pleaser is furnished without an antique in sight, paying homage to the town's agricultural (citrus) legacy with a bold industrial chic. World-inspired appetizers range from Hawaiian-style ahi poke to southeast Asian coconut shrimp tempura accented with spiced apricots. Main courses come from the Mediterranean (pasta and risotto), Mexico (*carne asada* with avocado-corn relish), the American south (authentic Louisiana gumbo), and your mom's kitchen (meatloaf smothered in gravy and fried onions). Gleaming bar shelves house myriad bottles for the extensive Martini menu, and outdoor foyer tables are nicely protected from the street.

122 No. Glassell St. (1/2 block north of Chapman), Orange. ✆ **714/639-9600.** Reservations recommended. Main courses $8–$13 lunch, $12–$24 dinner. AE, DC, MC, V. Tues–Sat 11:30am–3pm and 5–10pm.

Crab Cooker SEAFOOD   Since 1951, folks in search of fresh, well-prepared seafood have headed to this bright-red former bank building. Also a fish market, the Crab Cooker has a casual atmosphere of humble wooden tables, uncomplicated smoked and grilled preparations, and meticulously selected fresh fare. The place is especially proud of its Maryland crab cakes and recently added clams and oysters to the repertoire.

2200 Newport Blvd., Newport Beach. ✆ **949/673-0100.** Main courses $8–$19 lunch, $10–$25 dinner. AE, MC, V. Sun–Thurs 11am–9pm; Fri–Sat 11am–10pm.

INEXPENSIVE

Felix Continental Cafe ✿ CUBAN/SPANISH   If you like the recreated Disneyland Main Street, you'll love the historic 1886 town square in the city of Orange, on view from the cozy sidewalk tables outside the Felix Continental Cafe. Dining on traditional Cuban specialties (such as citrus-marinated chicken, black beans and rice, and fried plantains) and watching traffic spin around the magnificent fountain and rose bushes of the plaza evokes old Havana or Madrid rather than the cookie-cutter Orange County communities just blocks away. The food receives praise from restaurant reviewers and loyal locals alike.

36 Plaza Sq. (at the corner of Chapman and Glassell), Orange. ✆ **714/633-5842.** Reservations recommended for dinner. Main courses $6–$14. AE, DC, MC, V. Mon–Thurs 7am–9pm, Fri 7am–10pm, Sat 8am–10pm, Sun 8am–9pm.

Mrs. Knott's Chicken Dinner Restaurant ✿ *(Kids)* AMERICAN Knott's Berry Farm got its start as a down-home diner, and you can still get a hearty all-American meal without even entering the theme park. The restaurant that started it all, descended from Cordelia Knott's humble Depression-era farmland tearoom, stands just outside the park's entrance, with plenty of free parking for patrons. Looking just as you'd expect—country cute, with window shutters and paisley aplenty—the restaurant's featured attraction is the original fried chicken dinner, complete with soup, salad, buttermilk biscuits, mashed potatoes and gravy, and a slice of famous pie. Country fried steak, pot roast, roast turkey, and pork ribs are options, as well as sandwiches, salads, and a terrific chicken potpie. Boysenberries abound (of course!), from breakfast jam to traditional double-crust pies, and there's even an adjacent take-out shop that's always crowded.

8039 Beach Blvd. (near La Palma), Buena Park. ✆ **714/220-5080.** Reservations not accepted. Main courses $5–$7, complete dinners $10.95. AE, DC, DISC, MC, V. Sun–Thu 7am–8:30pm, Fri 7am–9pm, Sat 7am–9:30pm.

Just the Two of Us . . .

As parents know only too well, it's sometimes a challenge to find family-friendly dining—especially when vacationing in unfamiliar territory. But in Anaheim, where Disney-bound families make up a large percentage of all visitors, nearly every restaurant offers kid-appeal and is well versed in accommodating youngsters of all ages in even the most elegant eateries.

But what are the options for childfree travelers, or parents who stash the kids with in-hotel childcare for a night out? The challenge might be where to find an atmosphere conducive to romance; here are a few sure-fire suggestions for kindling sparks over a quiet dinner alone.

- Even though well-behaved kids are often spotted nibbling *foie gras* with the best of them, **Napa Rose** (p. 70) has architectural nuances and culinary details best appreciated by adults, who can relax and get re-acquainted at comfortably private tables looking out striking picture windows.

- With a serene Eastern ambiance, **Yamabuki** (p. 71) is a quiet temple of grown-up style and fine Japanese food—and remember, many delicacies that elicit up-turned noses in children have alluring, almost aphrodisiac qualities.

- At **The White House** (p. 77), a stately historic mansion's rooms provide an intimate setting for dinner, and twinkling candles and outdoor Tivoli lights enhance the mood.

3 In Los Angeles

L.A.'S WESTSIDE & THE BEACHES
EXPENSIVE

Chinois on Main ★ FRANCO-CHINESE Wolfgang Puck's Franco-Chinese eatery bustles nightly with locals and visitors who are wowed by the eatery's reputation and rarely disappointed by the food. Groundbreaking in its time, the restaurant still relies on the same quirky East-meets-West mélange of ingredients and technique. The menu is just about equally split between Chinois's signature dishes and new creations by head chef Makoto Tanaka. The most famous of the former are Cantonese duck in a sweet-tangy plum sauce, and farm-raised whole catfish that's perfectly deep-fried and dramatically presented. Terrific newer dishes include lobster and sea bass sautéed together and flavored with porcini oil and *ponzu* sauce, and rare roasted loin of venison served in a ginger-spiced port and sun-dried cherries sauce. Chef Tanaka will gladly prepare, on request, grilled squab on pan-fried noodles. This off-menu dish comes with a rich garlic-ginger sauce and sautéed shiitake and oyster mushrooms; it's said to be a favorite of regulars Luther Vandross and Shirley MacLaine. The dining room, designed by Puck's wife, Barbara Lazaroff, is as visually colorful as it is acoustically loud.

2709 Main St. (south of Pico Blvd.), Santa Monica. © 310/392-9025. Reservations required. Main courses $23–$29. AE, DC, MC, V. Wed–Fri 11:30am–2pm; daily 6–10:30pm. Valet parking $5.

The Lobster ☆ SEAFOOD

There's been a seafood shack called The Lobster on the Santa Monica Pier since 1923—almost as long as the pier's been standing—but 2000's revival brings a new sophistication to the old favorite. The interior is completely rebuilt, but still accentuates a bright seaside ambiance and million-dollar ocean view. Chef Allyson Thurber, who brings an impressive culinary pedigree (including downtown's Water Grill) to the kitchen, has revamped the menu. Ultra-fresh fish and thoughtful preparation are the hallmarks here, with choices that range from a namesake steamed live Maine lobster or spicy Louisiana prawns to sautéed North Carolina black bass luxuriating in white truffle sauce and accompanied by lobster salad. Creative appetizers include ahi carpaccio with tangy *tobiko* wasabi, steamed mussels and Manila clams with applewood bacon, and oysters plain or fancy. The menu offers a couple of fine steaks for landlubbers, and there's a practiced bar for dedicated imbibers.

1602 Ocean Ave. (at Colorado) © 310/458-9294. www.thelobster.com. Reservations recommended. Main courses $15–$32. AE, MC, V. Daily 11:30am–3pm and 5–10pm.

Valentino ☆☆ NORTHERN ITALIAN

Valentino is a good choice if you're splurging on just one special dinner. Charming owner Piero Selvaggio oversees two other restaurants, but his distinctive touch still pervades this 26-year-old flagship. This elegant spot continues to maintain its position as *Wine Spectator* magazine's top wine cellar, and former *New York Times* food critic Ruth Reichl calls this the best Italian restaurant in the U.S. The creations of Selvaggio and his brilliant young chef, Angelo Auriana, make dinners here lengthy multicourse affairs (often involving several bottles of wine). You might begin with a crisp *pinot grigio* paired with caviar-filled cannoli, or *crespelle,* thin little pancakes with fresh porcini mushrooms and a rich melt of fontina cheese. A rich *barolo* is the perfect accompaniment to rosemary-infused roasted rabbit; the fantastically fragrant risotto with white truffles is one of the most magnificent dishes we've ever had. Jackets are all but required in the elegant dining room.

3115 Pico Blvd. (west of Bundy Dr.), Santa Monica. ℂ 310/829-4313. www. welovewine.com. Reservations required. Main courses $22–$32. AE, DC, MC, V. Mon–Thurs 5:30–10:30pm; Fri 11:30am–2:30pm and 5:30–11pm; Sat 5:30–11pm. Valet parking $4.

MODERATE

Border Grill 𝄢𝄢𝄢 MEXICAN   Before Mary Sue Milliken and Susan Feniger spiced up cable TV as "Too Hot Tamales," they started this restaurant over in West Hollywood. Now Border Grill has moved to a boldly painted, cavernous (read: loud) space in Santa Monica, and the gals aren't in the kitchen here very much at all (though cookbooks and paraphernalia from their Food Network show are displayed prominently for sale). But their influence on the inspired menu is enough to maintain the cantina's enormous popularity with folks who swear by the authentic flavor of Yucatán fish tacos, rock shrimp with *ancho* chilies, and meaty *ropa vieja,* the traditional Latin stew. The best meatless dish is *mulitas de hongos,* a layering of Portobello mushrooms, *poblano* chilies, black beans, cheese, and guacamole, spiced up with roasted garlic and seared red chard. Distracting desserts are displayed prominently near the entrance, so you may spend the meal fantasizing about the yummy coconut flan or key lime pie.

1445 Fourth St. (between Broadway and Santa Monica Blvd.), Santa Monica. ℂ 310/451-1655. www.millikenandfeniger.com. Reservations recommended. Main courses $10–$21. AE, DC, DISC, MC, V. Mon 5–10pm; Tues–Thurs 11:30am–10pm; Fri–Sat 11:30am–11pm; Sun 11:30am–10pm.

Joe's 𝄢 AMERICAN ECLECTIC   This is one of West L.A.'s best dining bargains. Chef/owner Joe Miller excels in simple New American cuisine, particularly grilled fish and roasted meats accented with piquant herbs. Set in a tiny, quirky storefront, the humble room is a blank palette that belies Joe's popularity. The best tables are tucked away on the enclosed back patio. Lunch is a hidden treasure for those with a champagne palate but a seltzer pocketbook. Topping out at $15, all lunches include salad, one of Miller's exquisite soups, and especially prompt service. Beer and wine are served, except during weekday lunchtime (regulation, due to the elementary school across the street).

1023 Abbot Kinney Blvd., Venice. ☎ 310/399-5811. www.joesrestaurant.com. Reservations required. Lunch main courses $8–$15; dinner main courses $18–$25. AE, MC, V. Tues–Fri 11:30am–2:30pm and 6–10pm; Sat–Sun 11am–2:30pm and 6–11pm. Free street parking.

La Serenata Gourmet ☆☆ MEXICAN Westsiders rejoiced when this branch of Boyle Heights's award-winning La Serenata de Girabaldi began serving its authentic, but innovative, Mexican cuisine just a block away from the Westside Pavilion shopping center. This place is casual, fun, and intensely delicious. Specialties like shrimp enchiladas, fish tacos, and pork *gorditas* are all accented with hand-patted corn tortillas, fresh chips dusted with *antejo* cheese, and flavorful fresh salsas. Always packed to capacity, the restaurant finally expanded in 1998, but try to avoid the prime lunch and dinner hours nevertheless.

Adventurous diners head to the original La Serenata de Girabaldi, 1842 First St. (between Boyle and State Streets; ☎ 213/265-2887), reopened in 2000 after an extensive remodel. The menu is more formal, the ambiance is more authentic, and secured valet parking is provided for those worried about the sketchy neighborhood.

10924 W. Pico Blvd., West L.A. ☎ 310/441-9667. Main courses $8–$13. AE, MC, V. Daily 11am–3:30pm and 5–10pm (Fri–Sat until 10:30pm). Metered street parking.

INEXPENSIVE

The Apple Pan ☆☆ SANDWICHES/AMERICAN There are no tables, just a U-shaped counter, at this classic American burger shack and L.A. landmark. Open since 1947, the Apple Pan is a diner that looks—and acts—the part. It's famous for juicy burgers, bullet-speed service, and an authentic frills-free atmosphere. The hickory burger is best, though the tuna sandwich also has its huge share of fans. Ham, egg-salad, and Swiss cheese sandwiches round out the menu. Definitely order the fries and, if you're in the mood, the home-baked apple pie too.

10801 Pico Blvd. (east of Westwood Blvd.). ☎ 310/475-3585. Most menu items under $5. No credit cards. Tues–Thurs and Sun 11am–midnight; Fri–Sat 11am–1am.

Blueberry ☆ AMERICAN/BREAKFAST This Santa Monica cafe is popular among shoppers and locals from the surrounding laid-back beach community. It serves only breakfast and lunch—Blueberry's owner devotes the dinner hour to the über-trendy Rix around the corner. The setting is 1930s American farmhouse. From the blue bandana seat cushions to vintage music and print ads, from picket-fence railings to overalls-clad waitstaff, this place truly does evoke a Depression-era small-town diner. The food is a "square deal" too, starting with a basket of crispy-edged minimuffins (blueberry, of course) when you're seated, and including hearty egg dishes, waffles, and pancakes, plus generous lunch salads and sandwiches. But we'll bet Ma Kettle never used goat cheese or *pancetta* in *her* omelets. The menu is up-to-date and served with plenty of fresh-brewed gourmet-roasted coffee. Blueberry is tiny, with just a few tables on the main floor and cozy loft, so expect a wait during peak times.

510 Santa Monica Blvd. (at Fifth St.), Santa Monica. ✆ 310/394-7766. Main courses $4.50–$8. AE, MC, V. Daily 8am–3pm. Metered street parking.

Kay 'n Dave's Cantina MEXICAN *(Kids* A beach community favorite for "really big portions of really good food at really low prices," Kay 'n Dave's cooks with no lard and has a vegetarian-friendly menu with plenty of meat items too. Come early (and be prepared to wait) for breakfast, as local devotees line up for five kinds of fluffy pancakes, zesty omelets, or one of the best breakfast burritos in town. Grilled tuna Veracruz, spinach and chicken enchiladas in tomatillo salsa, seafood fajitas tostada, vegetable-filled corn tamales, and other Mexican specialties really are served in huge portions, making this a great choice to energize for (or reenergize after) an action-packed day of beach sightseeing. Bring the family—there is a kids' menu and crayons on every table.

262 26th St. (south of San Vicente Blvd.), Santa Monica. ✆ 310/260-1355. Reservations not accepted. Main courses $5–$10. AE, MC, V. Mon–Thurs 11am–9:30pm; Fri 11am–10pm; Sat 8:30am–10pm; Sun 8:30am–9:30pm. Metered street parking .

BEVERLY HILLS AND HOLLYWOOD
EXPENSIVE

Matsuhisa *(★★★* JAPANESE/PERUVIAN Japanese chef/owner Nobuyuki Matsuhisa arrived in Los Angeles via Peru and opened what may be the most creative restaurant in the entire city. A true master of fish cookery, Matsuhisa creates fantastic, unusual dishes by combining Japanese flavors with South American spices and salsas. Broiled sea bass with black truffles, sautéed squid with garlic and soy, and Dungeness crab tossed with chilies and cream are good examples of the masterfully prepared delicacies that are available in addition to thickly sliced *nigiri* and creative sushi rolls. Matsuhisa is perennially popular with celebrities and hard-core foodies, so reserve early for those hard-to-get tables. The small crowded main dining room suffers from poor lighting and precious lack of privacy; many big names are ushered through to private dining rooms. If you dare, ask for *omakase,* and the chef will personally compose a selection of eccentric dishes.

129 N. La Cienega Blvd. (north of Wilshire Blvd.), Beverly Hills. ✆ 310/659-9639. Reservations recommended. Main courses $14–$26; sushi $4–$13 per order; full omakase dinner from $65. AE, DC, MC, V. Mon–Fri 11:45am–2:15pm; daily 5:45–10:15pm. Valet parking $3.50.

Patina ⚜⚜⚜ CALIFORNIA-FRENCH Joachim Splichal, arguably L.A.'s best chef, is also a genius at choosing and training top chefs to cook in his kitchens while he jets around the world. Patina routinely wins the highest praise from demanding gourmands, who are happy to empty their bank accounts for unbeatable meals that almost never miss their intended mark. The dining room is straightforwardly attractive, low key, well lit, and professional, without the slightest hint of stuffiness. The menu is equally disarming: "Mallard Duck with Portobello Mushrooms" gives little hint of the brilliant colors and flavors that appear on the plate. The seasonal menu features partridge, pheasant, venison, and other game in winter and spotlights exotic local vegetables in warmer months. Seafood is always available; if Maine lobster cannelloni or asparagus-wrapped John Dory is on the menu, order it. Patina is justifiably famous for its mashed potatoes and potato-truffle chips; be sure to include one (or both) with your meal.

5955 Melrose Ave. (west of Cahuenga Blvd.). ✆ 323/467-1108. www. patina-pinot.com. Reservations required. Main courses $18–$30. AE, DC, DISC, MC, V. Sun–Thurs 6–9:30pm (Tues also noon–2pm); Fri 6–10:30pm; Sat 5:30–10:30pm.

Spago ⚜⚜⚜ CALIFORNIA Wolfgang Puck is more than a great chef, he's also a masterful businessman and publicist who has made Spago one of the best-known restaurants in the United States. Despite all the hoopla—and almost 20 years of service—Spago remains one of L.A.'s top-rated restaurants. Talented Puck henchman Lee Hefter presides over the kitchen, delivering the culinary sophistication demanded by an upscale Beverly Hills crowd. This high-style indoor/outdoor space glows with the aura of big bucks, celebrity, and the perfectly honed California cuisine that can honestly take credit for setting the standard. Spago is also one of the last places in L.A. where men will feel most comfortable in jacket and tie (suggested, but not required). All eyes may be on the romantically twinkle-lit outdoor patio (the most coveted tables), but the food takes center stage. You simply can't choose wrong—highlights include the appetizer of foie gras "three ways"; savory duck either honey-lacquered and topped with foie gras, or Cantonese-style with a citrus tang; and rich Austrian dishes from "Wolfie's" childhood, like spicy beef goulash or perfect veal schnitzel.

176 N. Canon Dr. (north of Wilshire). © 310/385-0880. www.wolfgangpuck.com. Reservations required. Main courses $18–$34 tasting menu $85. AE, DC, DISC, MC, V. Sun and Tues–Thurs 6–10pm; Fri–Sat 5:30–11pm.

MODERATE

Ca' Brea ✦✦ NORTHERN ITALIAN   When Ca' Brea opened in 1991, its talented chef/owner Antonio Tommasi was catapulted into a public spotlight shared by only a handful of L.A. chefs—Wolfgang Puck, Michel Richard, and Joachim Splichal. Since then, Tommasi has opened two other celebrated restaurants, Locanda Veneta in Hollywood and Ca' Del Sole in the Valley, but, for many, Ca' Brea remains tops. The restaurant's refreshingly bright two-story dining room is a happy place, hung with colorful, oversize contemporary paintings and backed by an open prep-kitchen where you can watch as your seafood cakes are sautéed and your Napa cabbage braised. Booths are the most coveted seats; but with only 20 tables in all, be thankful you're sitting anywhere. Detractors might complain that Ca' Brea isn't what it used to be since Tommasi began splitting his time between three restaurants, but he stops in daily and keeps a very close watch over his handpicked staff. Consistently excellent dishes include the roasted pork sausage, the butter squash-stuffed ravioli, and a different risotto each day—always rich, creamy, and delightfully indulgent.

346 S. La Brea Ave. (north of Wilshire Blvd.). © 323/938-2863. Reservations recommended. Main courses $9–$21; lunch $7–$20. AE, DC, MC, V. Mon–Fri 11:30am–2:30pm; Mon–Thurs 5:30–10:30pm; Fri–Sat 5:30–11pm. Valet parking $3.50.

Kate Mantilini ✦ AMERICAN   It's rare to find a restaurant that feels comfortably familiar yet cutting-edge trendy at the same time—and also happens to be one of L.A.'s few late-night eateries. Kate Mantilini fits the bill perfectly. One of the first to bring meatloaf back into fashion, Kate's offers a huge menu of upscale truck-stop favorites like "white" chili (made with chicken, white beans, and Jack cheese), grilled steaks and fish, a few token pastas, and just about anything you might crave. At 2am, nothing quite beats a bowl of lentil-vegetable soup and some garlic-cheese toast, unless your taste runs to fresh oysters and a dry martini—Kate has it all. The huge mural of the Hagler-Hearns boxing match that dominates the stark, open interior provides the only clue to the namesake's identity: Mantilini was an early female boxing promoter, around 1947.

9101 Wilshire Blvd. (at Doheny Dr.), Beverly Hills. ℭ **310/278-3699.** Reservations accepted only for parties of 6 or more. Main courses $7–$16. AE, MC, V. Mon–Thurs 7:30am–1am; Fri 7:30am–2am; Sat 11am–2am; Sun 10am–midnight. Validated valet parking.

Musso & Frank Grill ℛ AMERICAN/CONTINENTAL A survey of Hollywood restaurants that leaves out Musso & Frank is like a study of Las Vegas singers that fails to mention Wayne Newton. As L.A's oldest eatery (since 1919), Musso & Frank is the paragon of Old Hollywood grillrooms. This is where Faulkner and Hemingway drank during their screenwriting days and where Orson Welles used to hold court. The restaurant is still known for its bone-dry martinis and perfectly seasoned Bloody Marys. The setting is what you'd expect: oak-beamed ceilings, red-leather booths and banquettes, mahogany room dividers, and chandeliers with tiny shades. The extensive menu is a veritable survey of American/ Continental cookery. Hearty dinners include veal scaloppine Marsala, roast spring lamb with mint jelly, and broiled lobster. Grilled meats are a specialty, as is the Thursday-only chicken potpie. Regulars also flock in for Musso's trademark "flannel cakes," crêpe-thin pancakes flipped to order.

6667 Hollywood Blvd. (at Cherokee Ave.). ℭ **323/467-7788.** Reservations recommended. Main courses $13–$32. AE, DC, MC, V. Tues–Sat 11am–11pm. Self-parking $2.25 with validation.

Nyala ℛ ETHIOPIAN There are no fewer than four Ethiopian eateries along two compact blocks of Fairfax, but our favorite is Nyala; it's one of the larger ones, and probably the most popular. In a mellow setting—all earthen colors, tribal prints, and African music—an ethnically mixed crowd finds common ground in the expertly spiced (smoldering, rather than fiery) cuisine. For the uninitiated, Ethiopian food is a mosaic of chopped salads, chunky stews, and saucy vegetables, all served on a colorful enamel platter for communal enjoyment. There are no utensils, merely a basket of *injera,* the thick, tangy crepe used to scoop up the other food. Choices range from hearty chicken or lamb chunks stewed with tomatoes and onions to a parade of vegetarian choices (lentils, chick-peas, greens), each with a distinctive marinade. African beers and honey wine are perfect accompaniments.

1076 S. Fairfax Ave. (south of Olympic). © 323/936-5918. Reservations suggested. Main courses $8–$15. AE, DISC, MC, V. Daily 11:30am–11pm. Street parking.

INEXPENSIVE

El Cholo ⟨ℛ⟩ MEXICAN   There's authentic Mexican and then there's traditional Mexican—El Cholo is comfort food of the latter variety, south-of-the-border cuisine regularly craved by Angelenos. They've been serving it up in this pink adobe hacienda since 1927, even though the once-outlying mid-Wilshire neighborhood around them has turned into Koreatown. El Cholo's expertly blended margaritas, invitingly messy nachos, and classic combination dinners don't break new culinary ground, but the kitchen has perfected these standards over 70 years. We wish they bottled their rich enchilada sauce! Other specialties include seasonally available green-corn tamales and creative sizzling vegetarian fajitas that go way beyond just eliminating the meat. The atmosphere is festive, as people from all parts of town dine happily in the many rambling rooms that compose the restaurant. There's valet parking as well as a free self-park lot directly across the street.

Westsiders head to El Cholo's Santa Monica branch at 1025 Wilshire Blvd. (© **310/899-1106**).

1121 S. Western Ave. (south of Olympic Blvd.). © 323/734-2773. www.elcholo. com. Reservations suggested. Main courses $8–$14. AE, DC, MC, V. Mon–Thurs 11am–10pm; Fri–Sat 11am–11pm; Sun 11am–9pm. Free self-parking or valet parking $3.

Nate & Al ⟨ℛ⟩ DELI/BREAKFAST   If you want to know where old money rich-and-famous types go for comfort food, look no further. Despite its location in the center of Beverly Hills's "Golden Triangle," Nate & Al has remained unchanged since it opened in 1945, from the Naugahyde booths to the motherly waitresses, who treat you the same whether you're a house-account celebrity regular or just a visitor stopping in for an overstuffed pastrami on rye. Their too-salty chicken soup keeps Nate & Al from being the best L.A. deli (actually, we'd be hard pressed to choose any one deli as the city's best), but staples like chopped liver, dense potato pancakes, blintzes, borscht, and well-dilled pickles more than make up for it.

414 N. Beverly Dr. (at Brighton Way), Beverly Hills. © 310/274-0101. Main courses $8–$13. AE, DISC, MC, V. Daily 7:30am–9pm. Free parking with validation.

Pink's Hot Dogs *Kids* HOT DOGS   Pink's isn't your usual guide-book recommendation, but then again, this crusty corner stand isn't your usual doggery either. The heartburn-inducing chilidogs are craved by even the most upstanding, health-conscious Angelenos. Bruce Willis reportedly proposed to Demi Moore at the 59-year-old shack that grew around the late Paul Pink's 10¢ wiener cart. Pray the bulldozers stay away from this little nugget of a place.

709 N. La Brea Ave. (at Melrose Ave.). © 323/931-4223. www.pinkshollywood. com. Hot dogs $2.10. No credit cards. Sun–Thurs 9:30am–2am; Fri–Sat 9:30am–3am.

Roscoe's House of Chicken 'n' Waffles SOUTHERN/BREAKFAST   It sounds like a bad joke: Only chicken and waffle dishes are served here, a rubric that also encompasses eggs and chicken livers. Its close proximity to CBS Television City has turned this simple restaurant into a kind of de facto commissary for the network. A chicken-and-cheese omelet isn't everyone's ideal way to begin the day, but it's de rigueur at Roscoe's. At lunch, few calorie-unconscious diners can resist the chicken smothered in gravy and onions, a house specialty that's served with waffles or grits and biscuits. Large chicken-salad bowls and chicken sandwiches also provide plenty of cluck for the buck. Homemade corn bread, sweet-potato pie, homemade potato salad, and corn on the cob are available as side orders, and wine and beer are sold.

Roscoe's can also be found at 4907 W. Washington Blvd., La Brea Avenue (© **323/936-3730**), and 5006 W. Pico Blvd. (© **323/934-4405**).

1514 N. Gower St. (at Sunset Blvd.). © **323/466-7453**. Main courses $4–$11. No credit cards. Sun–Thurs 9am–midnight; Fri–Sat 9am–4am. Metered street parking.

THE SAN FERNANDO VALLEY
EXPENSIVE

Pinot Bistro *FF* CALIFORNIA/FRENCH   When the Valley crowd doesn't want to make the drive to Patina, they pack into Pinot Bistro, one of Joachim Splichal's other successful restaurants. The Valley's great bistro is designed with dark woods, etched glass, and cream-colored walls that scream "trendy French" almost as loudly as the rich, straightforward cooking. The menu, a symphony of California and continental elements, includes a beautiful warm potato tart with smoked whitefish, and baby lobster tails with creamy polenta—both studies in culinary perfection. The most popular dish here is chef Octavio Becerra's Frenchified Tuscan bean soup, infused with oven-dried tomatoes and roasted garlic and served over crusty *ciabatta* bread. The generously portioned main dishes continue the gourmet theme: baby lobster risotto, braised oxtail with parsley gnocchi, and puff pastry stuffed with bay scallops, Manila clams, and roast duck. The service is good, attentive, and unobtrusive. Many regulars prefer Pinot Bistro at lunch, when a less expensive menu is served to a more easygoing crowd.

12969 Ventura Blvd. (west of Coldwater Canyon Ave.), Studio City. ℂ 818/990-0500. www.patina-pinot.com. Reservations required. Main courses $7–$13 lunch, $16–$22 dinner. AE, DC, DISC, MC, V. Mon–Fri 11:30am–2:30pm; Mon–Thurs 6–10pm; Fri 6–10:30pm; Sat 5:30–10:30pm; Sun 5:30–9:30pm. Valet parking $3.50.

MODERATE

Jerry's Famous Deli ⋒ ⟮Kids⟯ DELI   Here's a simple yet sizable deli where the Valley's hipsters go to relieve their late-night munchies. This place probably has one of the largest menus in America—a tome that spans cultures and continents, from Central America to China to New York. From salads to sandwiches to steak-and-seafood platters, everything—including breakfast—is served all day. Jerry's is consistently good at lox and eggs, pastrami sandwiches, potato pancakes, and all the deli staples. It's also an integral part of L.A.'s cultural landscape and a favorite of the show-business types who populate the adjacent foothill neighborhoods. It even has a full bar.

12655 Ventura Blvd. (just east of Coldwater Canyon Ave.), Studio City. ℂ 818/980-4245. Dinner main courses $9–$14; breakfast $2–$11; sandwiches and salads $4–$12. AE, MC, V. Daily 24 hr. Free parking.

Katsu ⋒⋒⋒ JAPANESE   The latest entry onto Studio City's unofficial "Sushi Row" is no newcomer: Katsu Michite has been teaching Angelenos to love fine sushi for years, and many of the city's star sushi masters at places like R23 and the Hump are veterans of Katsu's much-missed Los Feliz flagship. Katsu's new venue is this stark, contemporary space accented with rough-cut wood and bamboo; in addition to the main dining room and intimate sushi counter, there's a smaller, hidden bar where Katsu-san delivers his unequaled *omakase* (chef's choice). Masterful touches distinguish Katsu's fare from its neighbors, things like fresh-grated wasabi, or respectfully decanted chilled sake. The sushi is always perfect and never fancy (look elsewhere for those trendy "inside-out" rolls), and there's a long menu of cooked delicacies like meltingly good grilled butterfish, satisfying tofu steak piled high with flaky bonito and shredded scallions, and outstanding crisp salmon skin salad.

On the other side of the hill, **Katsu 3rd** (8636 W. Third St.; (© **310/273-3605**) sits across the street from Cedars-Sinai and attracts a trendy, less food-serious crowd.

11920 Ventura Blvd. (east of Laurel Canyon), Studio City. © 818/760-4585. Reservations recommended. Main courses $9–$20; sushi $3–$7; *omakase* from $70 up. AE, MC, V. Mon–Fri 11:30am–2:30pm, daily 5–10:30pm. Valet parking $3.

Paul's Cafe 🍴🍴 CALIFORNIA/FRENCH   One of the Valley's hardest reservations (hint: call early, dine early, or both) is at this midsize neighborhood bistro, where a quietly elegant setting belies the friendly prices that have made Paul's a big success. Expect the seasonal menu to include plenty of seafood (roasted sea bass laid atop spinach with a mushroom vinaigrette, sautéed sea scallops with saffron risotto and lobster sauce), hearty meats (filet mignon with port sauce accompanied by a creamy sweet potato-Gorgonzola gratin, garlic-rubbed rack of lamb sweetened with mint), and appetizers that ought to be main courses (pepper crusted seared ahi drizzled with scallion vinaigrette, crab cakes with lobster *aioli*). Soup or a small salad is only $1 with any dinner, and locals love the mere $2 corkage fee. Paul's manages to be intimate enough for lovers yet also welcoming for families—its success is no surprise.

13456 Ventura Blvd. (between Dixie Canyon and Woodman Ave.), Sherman Oaks. © 818/789-3575. Main courses $12–$17 dinner, $8–$11 lunch. AE, MC, V. Mon–Thurs 11:30am–2:30pm and 5:30–10pm; Fri 11:30am–2:30pm and 5:30–11pm; Sat 5–11pm; Sun 5–9:30pm. Metered street parking or valet parking $4.

INEXPENSIVE

Casa Vega 🍴 MEXICAN   We believe that everyone loves a friendly dive, and Casa Vega is one of our local favorites. A faux-weathered adobe exterior conceals red Naugahyde booths lurking among fake potted plants and 1960s amateur oil paintings of dark-eyed Mexican children and cape-waving bullfighters. (The decor achieves critical mass at Christmas, when everything drips with tinsel.) Locals love this place for its good, cheap margaritas (order on the rocks), bottomless baskets of hot and salty chips, and traditional combination dinners, which all come with Casa Vega's patented tostada-style dinner salad. Street parking is so plentiful here you should use the valet only as a last resort.

13371 Ventura Blvd. (at Fulton Ave.), Sherman Oaks. © 818/788-4868. Reservations recommended. Main courses $5–$11. AE, DC, MC, V. Mon–Fri 11am–2am; Sat–Sun 4pm–2am. Metered street parking or $2.50 valet.

Du-par's Restaurant & Bakery 🍴AMERICAN/DINER   It's been called a "culinary wax museum," the last of a dying breed, the kind of coffee shop Donna Reed took the family to for blue-plate specials. This isn't a trendy new theme place, it's the real deal—and that motherly waitress who calls everyone under 60 "hon" has probably been slinging hash here for 20 or 30 years. Du-par's is popular among old-timers who made it part of their daily routine decades ago, show-business denizens who eschew the industry watering holes, a new generation that appreciates a tasty, cheap meal . . . well, everyone, really. It's common knowledge that Du-par's makes the best buttermilk pancakes in town, though some prefer the eggy, perfect French toast (extra-crispy around the edges, please). Mouth-watering pies (blueberry cream cheese, coconut cream, and more) line the front display case and can be had for a song.

West Hollywood denizens can visit the branch of Du-par's in the Ramada Hotel, 8571 Santa Monica Blvd., west of La Cienega (© 310/659-7009); they're open until 3am on weekends *and* have a full bar. There's another Du-par's in Los Angeles at the Farmers Market, 6333 W. 3rd St. (© 323/933-8446), but it doesn't stay open as late.

12036 Ventura Blvd. (1 block east of Laurel Canyon Blvd.), Studio City. © 818/766-4437. www.Dupars.com. All items under $11. AE, DC, DISC, MC, V. Sun–Thurs 6am–1am; Fri–Sat 6am–4am. Free parking.

6

What to See and Do at the Disneyland Resort

For more advice on structuring your visit and making the most of your days in the theme parks, please see chapter 2, "Planning Your Trip to the Disneyland Resort."

1 Essentials

GETTING INFORMATION IN ADVANCE

For information on **The Disneyland Resort,** including show schedules and ride closures that apply to the specific day(s) of your visit, call ✆ **714/781-4565** (automated information) or 714/781-7290 (to speak to Guest Relations). You can also find out everything you need to know about the Disneyland Resort online, beginning with the official site, **www.disneyland.com**, which contains the very latest information on park improvements and additions, plus special offers (sometime on airfare or reduced admission) and an interactive trip planner that lets you build a custom Disney vacation package.

ADMISSION PRICES & TICKETING

Admission to *either* Disneyland or California Adventure, including unlimited rides and all festivities and entertainment, is $43 for adults and children over 11, $41 for seniors 60 and over, $33 for children 3 to 11, and free for children under 3. Parking is $7. Three- and four-day "Park Hopper" passports are available, allowing you unlimited in-and-out privileges at *both* parks every day. Prices for adults/children are $111/$87 (3-Day) and $137/$107 (4-Day).

If you plan on arriving during a busy time (when the gates open in the morning, or between 11am and 2pm), purchase your tickets in advance and get a jump on the crowds at the ticket counters. Advance tickets may be purchased through Disneyland's Web site (www.disneyland.com), at Disney stores in the United States, or by calling the ticket mail order line (✆ **714/781-4043**).

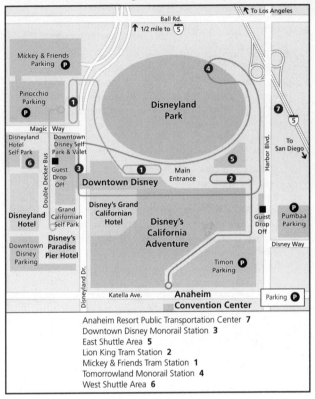

Anaheim Resort Public Transportation Center **7**
Downtown Disney Monorail Station **3**
East Shuttle Area **5**
Lion King Tram Station **2**
Mickey & Friends Tram Station **1**
Tomorrowland Monorail Station **4**
West Shuttle Area **6**

OPERATING HOURS

Disneyland and California Adventure are open every day of the year, but operating hours vary, so we recommend that you call for information that applies to the specific day(s) of your visit (© 714/781-4565). The same information, including ride closures and show schedules, can also be found online at **www.disneyland.com**. Generally speaking, the parks are open from 9 or 10am to 6 or 7pm on weekdays, fall to spring; and from 8 or 9am to midnight or 1am on weekends, holidays, and during winter, spring, or summer vacation periods.

The park's operating hours can give you some idea of what kinds of crowds Disney planners are expecting: the later the parks close, the more people will be there.

Tips **Relax . . . Think Fun, Not Frantic**

It's finally here, the dream vacation to the "Happiest Place on Earth!" Whether you're 6 or 60, it's hard to keep from getting caught up in the excitement, even when you're the one responsible for the (seemingly) endless planning stage.

Once you arrive and enter the theme park(s), kids—and plenty of adults—seem to kick into warp speed, but sensory overload doesn't mean you should abandon common sense. Here are just a few suggestions to avoid common pitfalls:

- **Write Down Your Car's Location:** When you're rushing to jump the tram for the park (see tip #3), it's easy to forget that your section/row/floor looks exactly like dozens of others in the parking lot or structure. Take a second to write down your parking location, because you'll be absorbing a lot of memories between now and the exhausted end of the day.

- **Don't Overplan:** Only the most stubbornly energetic park-goers (and if you have small children in tow, this is definitely not you) can manage to see everything at Disneyland in one day. California Adventure is more manageable, but can also be time-consuming at peak capacity. Agree as a group to several "must-do" rides and activities each day, so no one is disappointed by missing their favorite ride or attraction.

PARKING

The Disneyland Resort's enormous main parking structure on Disneyland Drive is difficult to miss; street signs are easy-to-see, and park employees direct traffic to available spaces. Frequent shuttles carry passengers to Disney's main entrance, (which is closest to Downtown Disney, but is the main entrance to all three areas) and to the Resort hotels. Parking is $7 per car for theme park visitors. Downtown Disney has a separate lot and offers validated parking (3 hours free; 5 hours with restaurant or theater validation).

FASTPASS

Many visitors tackle Disneyland (or California Adventure) systematically, beginning at the entrance and working their way clockwise around the park. But a better plan of attack is to arrive early and run

- **Pace Yourself:** First thing in the morning . . . why are those folks running to catch the parking lot tram? Relax, the theme parks aren't going anywhere, and trams run constantly during peak arrival and departure hours. While inside the park, stagger long waits in line with easy-entry shows and rides, and remember to sit with a refreshing drink every now and then. It may seem like a good idea to head right for another "must-do," but even the best ride is less fun if you've been cranky for 45 minutes in line.
- **Set a Spending Limit:** Kids should know they have a certain amount to spend on between-meal snacks and Disney souvenirs, so they'll look around and carefully decide which trinket is the one they can't live without.
- **Dress Comfortably:** We mean *really* comfortably, so you can stay that way throughout a long, hot day with lots of walking and lots of standing. Reliable walking shoes (sneakers or walking sandals are best), layered clothing (a sweatshirt or sweater for evening can be welcome, even in summer), and a hat and/or sunglasses to protect against sunburn are all must-haves.

to the most popular rides—the Indiana Jones Adventure, Star Tours, Space Mountain, Big Thunder Mountain Railroad, Splash Mountain, the Haunted Mansion, and Pirates of the Caribbean in Disneyland; and Soarin' Over California, Grizzly River Run, and It's Tough to be a Bug in California Adventure. Lines for these rides can last an hour or more in the middle of the day.

This time-honored plan of attack may eventually become obsolete, however, thanks to the new **FastPass** system. Here's how it works: Say you want to ride Space Mountain, but the line is long—*so* long the wait sign indicates a 75-minute standstill! Now the Automated FastPass ticket dispensers allow you to swipe the magnetic strip of your Disneyland entrance ticket, get a FastPass for later that day, and return to use the reduced-wait FastPass entrance. At press time, about ten Disneyland rides were equipped with FastPass;

several more will be added by the time you read this. The hottest features at California Adventure had FastPass built in from the start; for a complete list for each park, check your official map/guide when you enter.

BABY AND CHILD CARE

Located at the end of Main Street between the Camera Shop and First Aid, the **Baby Care Center** provides facilities for preparing formulas, warming bottles, nursing, and changing diapers. You can also find diaper machines and changing tables in many of Disneyland's restrooms. In California Adventure, there's a similarly outfitted Baby Center next to the Mission Tortilla Factory in the Pacific Wharf area.

Parents can rent **strollers** inside the parks; the daily rental fee is $7. They're available at Disneyland just inside the Main Entrance, and also in Tomorrowland at Star Trader. For California Adventure, stations are located inside the Main Entrance in Golden Gateway, and across from Soarin' Over California at Fly 'n' Buy.

LOCKERS   If you have any extra items you don't want to carry around the Disney parks, **lockers** are available for a $3 rental fee. At Disneyland, you'll find them next to the newsstand outside the Main Entrance, on Main Street U.S.A., and in Fantasyland (across from Toontown). At California Adventure, lockers are located outside the Main Entrance, and just inside the gates (in the Golden Gateway).

A Note on Shopping: Besides a selection of nationally recognized shops and boutiques—plus a few Disney exclusives—at Downtown Disney, each of the parks is filled with opportunities to pick up souvenirs, collectibles, and customized Disneyana. We've included just a few of the standouts in each park section below—the complete attraction maps you receive upon entry will list every shop and stand. Guests of the Disney Resort hotels should remember to take advantage of the purchase delivery service to avoid carrying packages throughout the park and onto rides.

For information on dining inside the theme parks, please refer to chapter 5, "Dining."

2 Touring Disneyland ✶✶✶

The Disneyland complex is divided into several theme "lands," each of which has a number of rides and attractions that are, more or less, related to that land's theme.

MAIN STREET U.S.A.

At the park's entrance, Main Street U.S.A. is a cinematic version of turn-of-the-century small-town America. The whitewashed Rockwellian fantasy is lined with gift shops, candy stores, a soda fountain, and a silent theater that continuously runs early Mickey Mouse films. Here you'll find the practical things you might need, such as stroller rentals and storage lockers.

Because there are no major rides, it's best to tour Main Street during the middle of the afternoon, when lines for rides are longest, and in the evening, when walkways can be packed with visitors viewing Disneyland's parades and shows. There's always something happening on Main Street; stop in at the information booth to the left of the Main Entrance for a schedule of the day's events.

Disneyland Railroad Trains were one of Walt Disney's favorite hobbies, and this calm ride was the first included in his Disneyland plan. With stations at Main Street, New Orleans Square, and Tomorrowland, the 19th-century steam engine offers a preview of the park as well as being a practical way to get around (especially during parades and shows when the center is packed with people). Between the Tomorrowland and Main Street stations, the train passes through an indoor diorama of the Grand Canyon—followed by "Primeval World," the Canyon, as it would have looked fifty million years ago.

The Walt Disney Story, Featuring "Great Moments With Mr. Lincoln" Thrill-seeking youngsters will consider this one a big ol' snore, but this tribute gallery illustrates the genesis of the Disney dynasty. Following a walkthrough retrospective on the life of Walter Elias Disney, guests are seated for a demonstration of Walt's first "audio-animatronic" display, an Abraham Lincoln monologue he created years before dreaming up the theme park that would employ his revolutionary technology in nearly every big-ticket ride. If you have a few free minutes, spend them here—you won't regret it.

MAIN STREET SHOPPING

Candy Kitchen Stroll by the glassed-in demonstration kitchen and watch as Disneyland's master confectioners create mouth-watering caramel apples, fudge, candy canes, and other delicacies before your very eyes. It's all available for purchase, everything from Rocky Road fudge to old-fashioned lemon drops.

Crystal Arts While it's not a practical choice for everyone, Disney's line of handcrafted crystal and glassware is unique, and can be

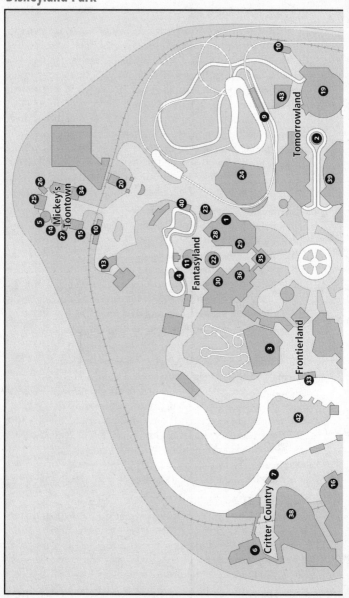

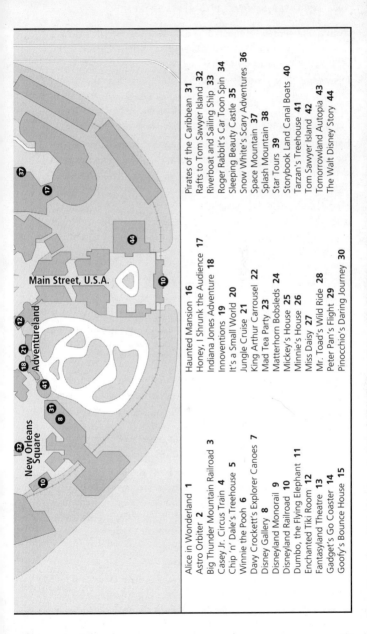

Main Street, U.S.A.

New Orleans Square

Adventureland

custom engraved or monogrammed. Check for special issue and limited edition pieces that commemorate various Disney grand openings, anniversaries, and so on.

Disneyana For those Disneyphiles who think they have everything, Disneyana is sure to offer some unexpected treasures with its collection of one-of-a-kinds and rare memorabilia. Sounds like hype, but this tiny shop often yields Ebay-worthy collectibles.

Emporium When it comes to finding that perfect souvenir try the park's largest logo store. From sportswear, collectible pins, and stationery to Disney-character plush animals and toys, there's something for everyone here.

Mad Hatter The largest of several all-hat shops throughout the park, the Mad Hatter features a great selection of character hats, including those ever-popular Mickey and Minnie ears. You can even get your name embroidered on any hat you purchase while you wait.

Penny Arcade Esmerelda, the fortune teller, welcomes you to an old-fashioned arcade, a carnival of flashing lights, music, and sound, where you can watch old movies through a hand-cranked slot machine, press your own Disneyland park souvenir pennies, or test your mettle with the oldie-but-goodie electric shock meter.

ADVENTURELAND

Inspired by the most exotic regions of Asia, Africa, India, and the South Pacific, Adventureland is the tropical corner of Disneyland. Because the subterranean Indiana Jones Adventure (see below) is squeezed into this otherwise small land, Adventureland can become crowded during high-volume periods, so expect close quarters.

Tarzan's Treehouse Kids can cavort inside this climb-around attraction based on Disney's animated film, complete with sound effects, surprises, and character appearances. Frequent visitors might recognize the former Swiss Family Treehouse, remodeled with vines and moss. The effect is usually lost on older and larger guests, who have to shimmy through some of the Treehouse's tight passageways.

Jungle Cruise ✻ One of the all-time Disney classics, this groaner of a ride has that predictable-yet-irresistible crusty charm of a George Burns comedy routine. Trained-to-be-corny boat operators lead riders on an *African Queen*-era trip down a tropical river inhabited by animatronic hippos, elephants, tribespeople; physically speaking, it's a tame ride, though first-timers can be easily startled—and little children will shriek with delight—as the boat swerves to avoid charging beasts or passes beneath jungle waterfalls.

Enchanted Tiki Room   Inside one of the most sedate attractions in Adventureland, you can sit and watch a 15-minute musical comedy featuring electronically animated tropical birds, flowers, and "tiki gods." Originally conceived as a Chinese restaurant with mealtime entertainment, the Tiki Room is the only ride in Disneyland with its own restrooms. Frequent visitors will notice the show is about 5 minutes shorter than a few years ago, a concession for the "MTV attention span."

Indiana Jones Adventure 🍴🍴🍴   Based on the Steven Spielberg films, Adventureland's star ride takes passengers into the Temple of the Forbidden Eye, in joltingly realistic all-terrain vehicles. Riders follow Indy and experience the perils of bubbling lava pits, whizzing arrows, fire-breathing serpents, collapsing bridges, and the familiar cinematic tumbling boulder (an effect that's very realistic in the front seats!). Disney Imagineers reached new heights with the design of this ride's line, which has so much detail throughout its twisting path that a half hour or more simply flies by.

ADVENTURELAND SHOPPING

The **Adventureland Bazaar, Tropical Imports,** and **South Seas Traders** sit side by side across from the Jungle Cruise, offering wares that include straw hats and bush jackets, replica African carvings and handicrafts, tropical resort wear and sandals, and even artificial shrunken heads and deadly snakes.

NEW ORLEANS SQUARE

A large, grassy green dotted with gas lamps, New Orleans Square evokes the French Quarter's timeless charm from antebellum mansions to sidewalk cafes and lakefront terraces. Jazz music wafts through the air, and portrait artists line a cobblestone alley of shops.

The Disney Gallery   Housed above Pirates of the Caribbean, the Disney Gallery, featuring archival paintings, models, and exhibits, is one of the park's hidden treasures. Stop in for a veritable cornucopia of Disney past, present, and future.

Haunted Mansion 🍴🍴🍴   One of Disney's must-see attractions since it opened in the late 1960s, this high-tech ghost house features illusions and tricks that never seem dated, plus some genuinely startling events and catchy tunes that'll make you want to ride again. Combining eerie walk-through halls with a meandering ride through the realm of "999 ghosts," the Haunted Mansion will even send you away with a hitchhiking apparition at your side.

Pirates of the Caribbean 🎫🎫🎫 This popular ride was the last personally overseen by Walt Disney, and it smacks of brilliant "imagineering." Visitors float on boats through mock underground caves, entering a world of swashbuckling, rum-running, and buried treasure. A pirate anthem and realistic village (inhabited by some of Disney's best audio-animatronic human and animal characters) help create a captivating Caribbean world. Though recently updated to remove some politically incorrect elements and tweak a few of the lower-tech effects, Pirates retains its classic appeal.

NEW ORLEANS SQUARE SHOPPING
Pieces of Eight Pirate gear from swords and buckles to skull-and-crossbones or three-point hats is available at this kitschy shop.

Disney Gallery Collectors Room Adjacent to the Disney Gallery, the shop has something for every budget: limited edition Disney lithographs and serigraphs, original artwork, collectibles, and postcards.

CRITTER COUNTRY
Critter Country is a sort of Frontierland without those pesky settlers. It's Disney's smallest land, out of the way and blessed with plenty of shade trees. Because most folks only pass through when riding Splash Mountain, it can be a cool and relaxing respite.

Davy Crockett's Explorer Canoes While it may not be the fastest ride in the park, this team-building row around Tom Sawyer Island is the only one where you actively control your boat (no underwater rails!) Hop into replica canoes, grab a paddle, and away you go. This ride is best when you have a large group, because no one likes to be (accidentally) splashed by a stranger!

Splash Mountain 🎫🎫🎫 This is one of the largest water flume rides in the world. Loosely based on the Disney movie *Song of the South*, the ride is lined with about 100 characters that won't stop singing "Zip-A-Dee-Doo-Dah." Be prepared to get wet, especially if someone sizable is in the front seat of your log-shaped boat.

CRITTER COUNTRY SHOPPING
In keeping with the "critter" theme, shopping here is limited to the **Briar Patch,** home to plush-toy versions of Critter Country characters and classic friends from throughout the park; and **Pooh**

Corner, your Winnie the Pooh headquarters carrying apparel, toys, books, jewelry, and other Pooh gift items.

FRONTIERLAND

Inspired by 19th-century America, Frontierland is an idealized version of pioneer days, from the early sternwheelers to western-themed shows, shops and eateries. On Saturdays, Sundays, and holidays, and during vacation periods, Frontierland's Rivers of America is home to the after dark Fantasmic! Show, which mixes magic, music, live performers, and special effects.

Just as he did in *The Sorcerer's Apprentice,* Mickey Mouse appears and uses his magical powers to create giant water fountains, enormous flowers, and fantasy creatures. There's pyrotechnics, lasers, and fog, as well as a 45-foot-tall dragon that breathes fire and sets the water of the Rivers of America aflame. For more information on Fantasmic!, see "After Dark in the Parks," in chapter 7).

Tom Sawyer Island 🎠   This do-it-yourself play area has balancing rocks, caves, a rope bridge, and a log fort. You get here by taking a raft across the river; there is no time limit, so you may explore as long as you want and return at your leisure (the island closes at dusk).

Big Thunder Mountain Railroad 🎠🎠   This Old West roller coaster is a runaway mine train that thunders through bat caves and caverns, past falling rocks and waterfalls; despite the unimposing setting, the ride is one of Disneyland's fastest roller coasters (enclosed tunnels might make this one for claustrophobes to avoid).

MICKEY'S TOONTOWN

This is a colorful, whimsical world inspired by the "Roger Rabbit" films—a wacky, gag-filled land populated by 'toons. It even looks like a cartoon come to life, a trippy, smile-inducing world without a straight line or right angle in sight. Younger visitors especially enjoy pushing all the buttons and playing with the gadgets found around every corner here; because of its popularity with families, Toontown is most crowded during the day but often deserted after dinnertime.

Jolly Trolley   This fun, roundabout ride from one end of Toontown to the other is a trolley that doesn't glide, but instead rolls, jiggles, and weaves along its wacky track.

Roger Rabbit's Car Toon Spin 🎠🎠   Climb into these round yellow taxicabs for an interactive ride that zigs, zags, swerves, slides, and simulates spinning out of control. Although you don't actually drive the cab, by turning the steering wheel you can control the direction the cab is pointing, so you can experience something different every time. This is the only ride that really sees long lines in Toontown, but the waiting areas are nearly as interesting as the ride.

TOONTOWN SHOPPING

Gag Factory/Toontown Five and Dime These interconnected stores form a offer souvenirs, apparel, plush toys, and favorites from Mickey Mouse and his friends. It's a great place to pickup less expensive souvenirs for the younger set, as well as gag gifts like a wedding veil and top hat that have mouse ears peeking through.

FANTASYLAND

Through the entrance to Sleeping Beauty Castle waits a fairy-tale world occupied by favorite storybook characters. Dedicated to the young at heart, Fantasyland brings to life a world of make-believe; a land where dreams really do come true. There are numerous short rides that cater to the under-6 set—including themed adventures featuring the classic Disney characters Snow White, Cinderella, Peter Pan, Casey Jr., Dumbo, Mr. Toad, Alice in Wonderland and Pinocchio—in addition to the attractions listed below.

King Arthur Carousel Featuring restored steeds from historic turn-of-the-(20th)century carousel, this cheery, colorful merry-go-round sits at the center of Fantasyland; despite modern high-tech rides all around, its appealing pipe organ and old-fashioned charm have a timeless appeal even for today's youngsters.

It's a Small World 𝒜 This indoor river ride through a panorama of children around the world features that catchy tune everybody loves to hate, sung in dozens of languages—but long lines stand as testament to the ride's ability to delight younger visitors. Outside, pastel castle spires and manicured gardens provide a pleasant waiting area, where every quarter hour a larger than life clock chimes and sets off an elaborate automated doll parade.

Matterhorn Bobsleds 𝒜𝒜 Disney's original roller coaster is this zippy ride through chilled caverns and drifting fog banks, all contained in the distinctive mountain whose summit is visible from the freeway (and is a pretty respectable scale model of the real Matterhorn in Switzerland). Despite being surpassed by more high-tech generations of coasters, the sharp turns and excellent views of this oldie-but-goodie have kept it on everyone's must-do lists.

FANTASYLAND SHOPPING

In addition to the specialty shops, you'll find a conventional **Toy Shop** and another outpost of the popular **Mad Hatter** hat shop (with custom stitching service available while you wait).

The Princess Boutique   Fulfilling many a little girl's dream of being a princess, this sugar-and-spice boutique carries costumes, jewelry, slippers, and magic wands to complete the transformation.

Villain's Lair   This wicked collection of merchandise celebrates Disney doers of evil deeds; our favorite classic villains. From hats and watches to costumes and artwork, there's something for everyone's inner dark side here.

TOMORROWLAND

Conceived as an optimistic look at the future, Tomorrowland employs an angular, metallic look popularized by futurists like Jules Verne. The original Tomorrowland opened with now-dated attractions like Mission to the Moon (later Mission to Mars, then scrapped entirely). The section was fully redesigned in the late '90s; in addition to the attractions listed below, you'll also find **Innoventions,** an interactive pavilion of near-future technology. Innoventions is close to what Disney envisioned for Tomorrowland, when he created exhibits like "House of the Future" and "Bathroom of Tomorrow" that showcased imaginative technology of the day.

Astro Orbiter   It looks like a glimmering geometric sculpture tower at the entrance to Tomorrowland, but it's also a spinning rocketship ride that's tame enough for even the youngest astronauts (though they must have adult accompaniment).

Autopia ★★   One of the 20 original attractions at Disneyland, the Autopia cars captured America's fascination with the "freeways" just beginning to punctuate the landscape, and offered a chance to climb behind the wheel to cruise curving highways in custom-built mini-cars. One of the most frequently redesigned rides, a new and improved Autopia was introduced in 2000, with updated cars, and extended track, and interactive "road hazards" along the way.

"Honey, I Shrunk the Audience"   Based on the popular movie series—featuring Rick Moranis in the role of Wayne Szalinski—this 3-D interactive movie is quite an impressive show, giving audience members the realistic sensation of having shrunk to thumbnail size. How interactive is the movie? We don't want to give anything away, but if mice and snakes frighten you, be on your guard . . .

Monorail Conceived as an example of futuristic public transportation, the classic Monorail elevated tram has stations in Tomorrowland and in Downtown Disney (the former Disneyland Hotel station). It's a sleek and quiet ride offering views of the entire Disneyland Resort; guests disembarking at Downtown Disney can have their hands stamped to re-enter Disneyland later in the day.

Space Mountain ☆☆☆ This pitch-black indoor roller coaster is one of the most innovative from Disney, a wild outer space ride that assaults your equilibrium with sharp turns, sudden drops, and ear-flattening speed. It also garners the park's most insistent warnings about who should not ride: those with heart, back, or neck problems, expectant mothers, people prone to motion sickness, very young children, strobe-sensitive visitors—hopefully that didn't describe you, because this ride rocks!

Star Tours ☆☆ This Disney-George Lucas joint venture is based on the *Star Wars* movies and stars droids C-3PO and R2-D2 (trivia buffs will love knowing that's the actual C-3PO from the film greeting riders during the "pre-show"). Using a 40-passenger flight simulator, the ride sends guests on a warp-speed misadventure achieved with wired seats and video effects.

TOMORROWLAND SHOPPING

You'll find an Autopia souvenir shop with miniature cars and automotive-themed toys, plus **Hatmosphere,** yet another Disney hat shop in case the need for mouse ears strikes suddenly (with custom stitching service available while you wait).

Star Trader If you're looking to avoid the end-of-day crush at Main Street's Emporium, this cavernous store is a great choice because they carry much of the same Disney merchandise, from sportswear, stationery, and hats to glassware, watches, and Tomorrowland-themed collectibles.

3 Touring California Adventure ☆☆

With a grand entrance designed to resemble one of those "Wish you were here" scenic postcards, California Adventure starts out with a bang. Beneath a scale model of the Golden Gate Bridge (watch carefully, the monorail passes overhead), handmade tiles of across-the-state scenes glimmer on either side. Just inside, **Sunshine Plaza** is anchored by an enormous gold titanium "sun" that shines all day, illuminated by computerized heliostats that follow the real sun's path. From this point, visitors can head into three themed areas,

---

Fun Fact **The Art of Building a Theme Park**

Disney designers and Imagineers have gotten somewhat more esoteric in recent years, and no one's sure whether the public will respond with praise—or even notice. While highly skilled yet anonymous staffers have historically constructed most of Disneyland, the plans for Disney's recent expansion called for skilled California artisans to create one-of-a-kind works of art. Examples include the tiled murals that sweep, wavelike, across either side of the California Adventure entry plaza—depicting representative scenes of the state; each was handmade by a team of Bay Area artists. Inside Disney's Grand Californian Hotel, the work of master craftspeople can be seen at the registration desk: Hand-cast blocks feature bears and other wildlife, Native American weavings serve as wall hangings, and individually crafted bronze Arts & Crafts replica lamps grace the long counter. Park staff gives tours of the hotel, see chapter 1, "The Best of Disneyland."

---

each containing rides, interactive attractions, live-action shows, and plenty of dining, snacking, and shopping opportunities. Two parades wind through the park, including the resurrected—and renamed—Disney's Electrical Parade (see "After Dark in the Parks," in chapter 7).

SHOPPING IN SUNSHINE PLAZA

Greetings from California   The main souvenir shop of California Adventure, this rambling series of rooms is packed with logo items, mementos, clothing, recreational supplies (the California Adventure beach towels are our favorite) and one of Disney's more appealing selection of gifts for the folks back home. *Tip:* Even if you're inspired to buy upon entering, have them hold your purchases—or deliver them to your Disney hotel room—for when you're ready to leave.

THE GOLDEN STATE

This area represents California's history, heritage, and physical attributes. Sound boring? Actually, the park's splashiest attractions are here, contained in a series of "sub-areas" that highlight different regions of the state: "Condor Flats" is a tribute to aviators; "Grizzly Peak" is the snow-dusted bear-shaped mountain (seen in the California Adventure logo) that towers over an 8-acre mini-wilderness; "Pacific Wharf's" boardwalk and waterfront ambiance was inspired

Disney's California Adventure

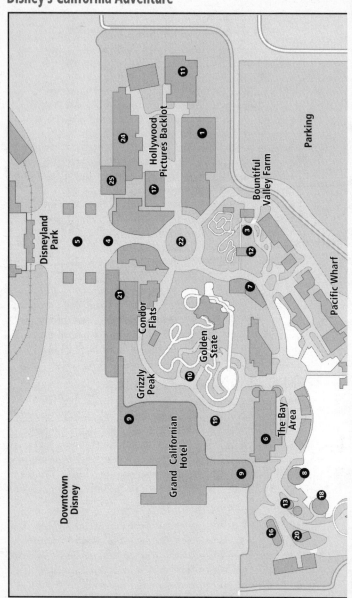

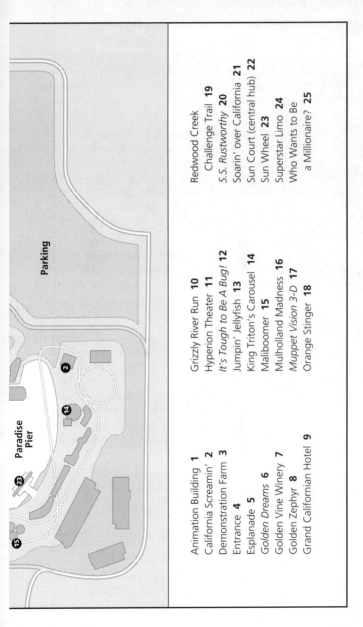

Paradise Pier

Parking

by Monterey's Cannery Row; the "Bountiful Farm" was dreamt up by Disney CEO Michael Eisner to pay tribute to California's agriculture; the "Bay Area" replicates San Francisco's gardens, Victorian architecture, Art Deco stylings and winding streets; and the Robert Mondavi "Golden Vine Winery" boasts a demonstration vineyard, Mission-style "aging room" (with a presentation on the art of winemaking).

Soarin' Over California 🎡🎡🎡   Set inside a weathered corrugated test-pilots' hangar, this is the ride that immediately rose to the top on everyone's run-to-get-in-line-first list (it's equipped with FastPass, but often reaches capacity by midday anyway). It uses cool cutting-edge technology to combine suspended seats with a spectac-ular IMAX-style surround-movie—so riders realistically "hang glide" over California's scenic wonders.

Grizzly River Run 🎡🎡   Up a clattering 300-foot long gold-ore conveyor, eight-passenger rafts are lifted to the drop-off for this splashy gold-country ride through caverns, mineshafts, and water-slides; it culminates with a wet plunge into a spouting geyser.

Redwood Creek Challenge Trail   This forest playground with smokejumper cable slides, net climbing, and swaying bridges is designed to give kids a fun workout.

"Golden Dreams" *Overrated*   Shown in the domed Golden Theater created specifically for the film (theater walls come alive with special effects during pivotal scenes), this 70mm 20-minute film celebrates the people and events that helped shape the character of California, from the days of Indian settlers, through immigrant arrival and on to the present day. It's an admirable idea—Whoopie Goldberg is the narrator and no expense was spared on historic reenactments—but the film might be too educational for most fun-seeking Disney goers.

Boudin Sourdough Bakery, Mission Tortillas, and **Lucky Fortune Cookies** 🎡   These distinctively Californian workplace attractions are like an excerpt from those elementary school field trips: Genuine equipment churning out genuine products (and sample tastes for observers) along with a brief history of the signifi-cance of each food. If you get hungry, each has a food counter where you can enjoy soup-in-a-sourdough-bowl; tacos, burritos, and enchiladas; and teriyaki bowls, egg rolls, and wonton soup.

"It's Tough To Be A Bug" 🎡🎡🎡   Using 3-D technology, *A Bug's Life* characters Flik and Hopper lead the audience on an underground romp with bees, termites, grasshoppers, stink bugs, spiders, and a few surprises that keep everyone hopping, ducking, and laughing along. Despite the G-rated image, this inventive and interactive experience is one of California Adventure's best features.

GOLDEN STATE SHOPPING

Condor Flats's **Fly 'n' Buy** offers souvenirs for aviation enthusiasts, from model airplanes to flight jackets and plenty of Disney logo items. If the wilderness theme of Grizzly Peak inspired you to plan a real outdoor adventure, **Rushin' River Outfitters** sells gear for snowboarding, ice climbing, kayaking, mountain biking, and so on. At the Bountiful Valley Farm, **Santa Rosa Seed & Supply** sells farming tools and supplies, while fresh produce and fruit are available farmer's market-style for healthful snacks. The Golden Vine Winery's **Wine Country Market** is a combination deli and gift shop featuring wine accessories and gourmet items.

PARADISE PIER

Journey back into the glory days of California's beachfront amusement piers—Santa Monica, Santa Cruz, Belmont Park—on this fantasy boardwalk. There are all the familiar boardwalk games (with stuffed prizes), small-scale carnival-style rides (in addition to the full-size attractions listed below) fast foods like pizza, corn dogs, and burritos.

California Screamin' 🎠🎠🎠   This classic roller coaster replicates the whitewashed wooden white-knucklers of the past—but with state-of-the-art steel construction and a smooth, computerized ride. An enormous Mickey Mouse silhouette provides the backdrop for a shriek-inducing loop-de-loop.

Maliboomer 🎠🎠   The 'Boomer's trio of towers (depicting giant strongman sledgehammer tests) catapult riders to the tip-top bell, then lets them down bungee-style with dangling feet.

Orange Stinger 🎠🎠   Individual bumblebee swings whoosh around inside an enormous, 4-story high orange whose spiral peel opens to the outside; this ride's surprise element wafts out—orange scent piped in to enhance the effect.

Mulholland Madness   Taking its cue from L.A.'s precarious hilltop street, this ride takes you on a winding, obstacle-ridden drive against a backdrop of murals depicting the Santa Monica Mountains.

Disney Dossier

Believe it or not, the Happiest Place on Earth keeps more than a few skeletons—as well as some just plain interesting facts—in its closet. For instance, did you know:

• Disneyland was carved out of **orange groves,** and the original plans called for carefully chosen individual trees to be left standing and included in the park's landscaping. On groundbreaking day, July 21, 1954, each tree in the orchard was marked with a ribbon—red to be cut and green to be spared. But the bulldozer operator went through and mowed down every tree indiscriminately . . . no one realized that he was color-blind.

• Disneyland designers utilized forced perspective in the construction of many of the park's structures to give the illusion of height and dramatic proportions while keeping the park a manageable size. The buildings on **Main Street U.S.A.,** for example, are actually 90% scale on the first floor, 80% on the second, and so forth. The stones on Sleeping Beauty Castle are carved in diminishing scale from the bottom to the top, giving it the illusion of towering height.

• The faces of the **Pirates of the Caribbean** were modeled after some of the early staff of Walt Disney Imagineering, who also lent their names to the second-floor "businesses" along Main Street U.S.A.

• Walt Disney maintained two apartments inside Disneyland. His apartment above the **Town Square** Fire Station has been kept just as it was when he lived there.

• The horses on Fantasyland's **King Arthur Carousel** are between 100 and 120 years old; Walt Disney found them

Sun Wheel ⭐⭐ This is the one everyone talks about, the ride-within-a-Ferris-wheel. Modeled after a 1927 Coney Island ride, the wheel features the traditional stationary gondolas around the perimeter, plus cars that ride on interior rails so they slide inward and outward with the centrifugal force of the wheel's rotational movement. Don't worry, you can choose which ones to climb into!

The other attractions at Paradise Pier include **King Triton's Carousel** (a merry-go-round featuring aquatic creatures), the kiddie lying in storage at Coney Island in New York and brought them to California to be cleaned and restored.

- **It's a Small World** was touted at its opening as "mingling the waters of the oceans and seas around the world with Small World's Seven Seaways." This was more than a publicity stunt—records from that time show such charges as $21.86 for a shipment of seawater from the Caribbean.
- **Indiana Jones: Temple of the Forbidden Eye,** Disneyland's subterranean thrill ride, won't be experienced the same way by any two groups of riders. Like a sophisticated computer game, the course is programmed with so many variables in the action that there are 160,000 possible combinations of events.
- When **Splash Mountain** had only 24 hours of operational testing under its belt, Disney CEO Michael Eisner insisted on taking a not-so-dry run. Since engineers hadn't yet adjusted the flume on the ride's signature splash, Eisner donned an unglamorous trash bag—with a hole cut through for his head—to protect him from a drenching, and boarded with several Imagineers. His response after the ride, "Can we go again?"
- Despite Disneyland's teetotaling reputation, the oft-rumored private **Club 33** has stood unobtrusively next to the Blue Bayou restaurant since 1967, when Walt Disney created the dining room/cocktail lounge for hosting sponsors, celebrities, and wealthy guests. It's easy to spot the door labeled "33", but harder to sneak a peek; you must be invited by a member, each of whom typically pays at least $10,000 to join.

ride **Jumpin' Jellyfish**, hands-on kids' playzone **S.S. rustworthy**, and retro "spinning spaceships" of **The Golden Zephyr**.

PARADISE PIER SHOPPING
Souvenir 66 is the Pier's most unique store, a replica roadside stand with a variety of travel and tourism-themed gifts, sundries, and collectibles for the Disney aficionado and nostalgic California lover. Other choices include **Treasures in Paradise** and **Sideshow**

Shirts, where trinkets, toys, beach-themed merchandise, and Paradise Pier souvenirs can be found.

HOLLYWOOD PICTURES BACKLOT

If you've visited Disney in Florida, you'll recognize elements of this *tromp l'oueil* recreation of a Hollywood movie studio lot. Pass through a studio archway flanked by gigantic golden elephants, and you'll find yourself on a surprisingly realistic "Hollywood Boulevard." The **ABC Soap Opera Bistro** leads a bevy of dining options, where you can dine in replica sets from your favorite soap operas (see "Other Dining Inside the Parks," in chapter 5).

Disney Animation   Inside this Art Deco building, visitors can participate in six different interactive galleries—learn how stories become animated features; watch Robin Williams become an animated character; listen to a Disney illustrator invent "Mushu", from *Mulan;* and even take a computerized personality test to see which Disney character *you* resemble most.

Hyperion Theater   Patterned after the historic Los Angeles Theater, this 2,000-seat showplace features live entertainment. When the park opened, the show was "Steps in Time," a tribute to classic Disney films; at press time, there was a new production in development.

Superstar Limo   The only riding attraction in the Backlot is this whimsical land, where you're cast as a hot new star being chauffeured around Hollywood to sign a big movie deal; the wacky but tame ride winds through Malibu, Rodeo Drive, Beverly Hills, and the Sunset Strip.

Jim Henson's MuppetVision 3D 👓👓   An on-screen blast from the past featuring Kermit, Miss Piggy, Gonzo, Fozzie Bear—and even hecklers Waldorf and Statler—this movie combines audio-animatronics, 3D and 70mm film technology, and the talents of Jim Henson disciples.

Who Wants To Be A Millionaire—Play It!   Hollywood Pictures Backlot's newest attraction (opened in September, 2001), is a play-long version of the popular TV gameshow, complete with the dramatic lighting and high tech set. Players compete for points, winning prizes ranging from collectible pins, T-shirts, hats and a trip. The live show is approximately 25 minutes in length, and runs once an hour in a 600-seat studio, and is a FASTPASS attraction.

HOLLYWOOD PICTURES BACKLOT SHOPPING

Directly adjacent to the ABC Soap Opera Bistro, **ABC Soaplink** is soap-fan-central, where you can buy collectible merchandise from various daytime dramas; TV monitors screen highlight reels of memorable weddings, cat fights, fatal diagnoses and break-ups. Other Backlot stores feature products that spoof current celebrity trends like designer pet products and *feng shui* kits, or silly jokes and magic supplies in a replica prop shop.

DOWNTOWN DISNEY ℛ

Borrowing a page from Central Florida's successful Disney compound, **Downtown Disney** is a district filled with restaurants, shops, and entertainment for all ages. Whether you want to stroll with kids in tow, have an upscale dinner-for-two, or party into the night, this colorful and sanitized "street scene" provides a venue. The promenade begins at the park gates and stretches toward the Disneyland Hotel; there are nearly 20 shops and boutiques, and a dozen-plus restaurants, live music venues, and entertainment options.

Highlights include **House of Blues,** the blues-jazz restaurant/club that features Delta-inspired cuisine and big-name music; **Ralph Brennan's Jazz Kitchen,** a spicy mix of New Orleans traditional foods and live jazz; **ESPN Zone,** the ultimate sports dining and entertainment experience, including an interactive game room; and **Y Arriba! Y Arriba!** where Latin cuisine combines with spicy entertainment and dancing; For more information on menus and prices for Downtown Disney restaurants and clubs, please refer to chapter 5, "Dining," and chapter 7, "After Dark Entertainment & Nightlife."

The most spectacular venue of the Downtown Disney shopping scene is **World of Disney,** one of the biggest Disney shopping experiences anywhere, with a vast range of logo items, keepsakes, toys, collectibles, and other souvenirs. It's an easy place to get lost—and the best place to do your gift shopping for everyone from infants to in-laws. Don't miss the two-story "wall of plush"—15,000 stuffed toys. Also worth a visit is the mall's other Disney-themed store, **Marceline's Confectionery,** patterned after the old-style candy emporium in Walt Disney's home town of Marceline, Missouri. Though the ambience is sleekly modern, the goods are hand-made and alluringly presented, as new-fangled sweets (flower-shaped sugars in terra cotta pots, taffeta gift boxes, and luscious truffles) share space with old-style treats (striped candy ribbons, ribbon-tied bags of chewy caramels, and a wall of jelly beans). Outside the shop, plate-glass windows let you watch them making fudge, caramel apples, and cookies in the open candy kitchen.

The rest of Downtown Disney's selection of stores and boutiques offers a little something for everyone, including **LEGO Imagination Center,** where small play stations are set up throughout a store filled with all things LEGO. A comprehensive selection of LEGO building sets is joined by unique-to-SoCal "LEGO Anaheim" and LEGOLAND California logo items, plus the LEGO Studios & Steven Spielberg MovieMaker set, featuring a PC camera and editing software to make your own Lego movies.

Compass Books & Cafe is a branch of the respected Northern California independent chain Books, Inc. whose socially conscious neighborhood bookstores are tailored to each location. The Anaheim store is well stocked for its size, with bestsellers, buzzed-about small-press books, and a selection of regional titles. Outside in the mall, Compass's magazine kiosk stocks an array of periodicals—in addition to every major name, you'll find foreign papers and mags, plus special interest titles in all categories.

The ultimate chick-magnet is **Sephora,** the European beauty superstore. Walls and aisles of sleekly displayed help-yourself fragrances and cosmetics are patrolled by trendy black-clad staff; nearly 200 brands range from Guerlain and Clinique to Urban Decay and Hard Candy.

Other mall-style boutiques feature bath and body products, surf/ skatewear for teens, wristwatches and timepieces, candles and home decor, Hollywood collectibles, island-themed resort wear, artisan-crafted sterling silver jewelry, and more.

Even if you're not staying at one of the Disney hotels, Downtown Disney is worth a visit. Locals and day-shoppers take advantage of the no-gate free entry and validated Downtown Disney parking lots (3 hours free; 5 with restaurant or theater validation).

4 Other Diversions in Orange County

Bowers Museum of Cultural Art ★★   This Santa Ana museum celebrates the diversity of the human family by showcasing the arts of world cultures. Presentations are as varied as a retrospective of Remington and fellow Western artists; an exhibit of the Dead

Downtown Disney

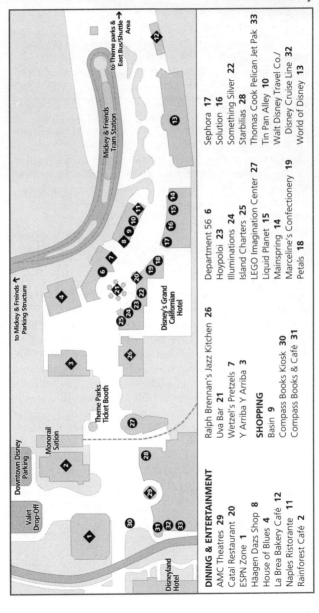

Downtown Disney Parking

Monorail Station

Valet Drop-Off

Disneyland Hotel

to Mickey & Freinds Parking Structure ←

Theme Parks Ticket Booth

Mickey & Friends Tram Station

to Theme parks & East Bus/Shuttle Area →

Disney's Grand Californian Hotel

DINING & ENTERTAINMENT

AMC Theatres **29**
Catal Restaurant **20**
ESPN Zone **1**
Häagen Dazs Shop **8**
House of Blues **4**
La Brea Bakery Café **12**
Naples Ristorante **11**
Rainforest Café **2**
Ralph Brennan's Jazz Kitchen **26**
Uva Bar **21**
Wetzel's Pretzels **7**
Y Arriba Y Arriba **3**

SHOPPING

Basin **9**
Compass Books Kiosk **30**
Compass Books & Café **31**
Department 56 **6**
Hoypoloi **23**
Illuminations **24**
Island Charters **25**
LEGO Imagination Center **27**
Liquid Planet **15**
Mainspring **14**
Marceline's Confectionery **19**
Petals **18**
Sephora **17**
Solution **16**
Something Silver **22**
Starbilias **28**
Thomas Cook Pelican Jet Pak **33**
Tin Pan Alley **10**
Walt Disney Travel Co./
  Disney Cruise Line **32**
World of Disney **13**

Tips Knott Here?

Full information and visiting tips for Knott's Berry Farm (and its new water park Knott's Soak City U.S.A.)—in nearby Buena Park—can be found in chapter 8, "Other Southern California Family Attractions."

Sea Scrolls and Holy Land photographs; and artifacts from China's "Forbidden City" Imperial Palace. The Bowers is one of those scholarly-yet-compelling institutions you might not have heard of, but that carries much weight in the art world. It's always worth seeing what's on the exhibit calendar, since it's just a short freeway hop from Anaheim. The adjacent Kidseum provides a hands-on cultural arts experience for children, providing stimulation and learning in an entertaining atmosphere.

2002 N. Main St., Santa Ana. ✆ 714/567-3600. Fax 714/567-3603. www.bowers. org. General admission (permanent exhibit) $5, free to kids under 5; tickets for special exhibitions $10–$16. Tues–Sun 10am–4pm.

Crystal Cathedral ✪ Designed by famed architect Philip Johnson, this angular, shimmering church is an architectural oddity that's been described as "the most spectacular religious edifice in the world." Hyperbole aside, you've never seen anything like it, and it's grander from the inside. The cathedral represents a four-pointed star, with 10,000 panes of glass covering the weblike, translucent walls and ceiling. Opened in 1980, the Crystal Cathedral is the pulpit for televangelist Robert Schuller, who broadcasts sermons and hymns to an audience of millions. The annual *Glory of Christmas* and *Glory of Easter* pageants feature live animals, floating "angels," and other grand theatrics.

12141 Lewis St., Garden Grove. ✆ 714/971-4000. Fax 714/750-3836. www. crystalcathedral.org. Tours Mon–Sat 9am–3:30pm.

Discovery Science Center ✪✪ Dubbed as the "amusement park for your mind," this modern-looking building is distinguished outside by a cosmic-looking cube standing askew (noticeable from the freeway) and on the inside by provocative hands-on exhibits, live science shows, and a 3-D laser theater. The 59,000-square-foot learning facility designed to spark children's natural curiosity, and kids are encouraged to touch, play, and explore the exhibits.

2500 N. Main St., Santa Ana. ☎ **714/542-CUBE.** Fax 714/542-2828. www. discoverycube.org. Admission $11 adults, $8.50 seniors 55+ and kids 3–17, 2 and under free. Daily 10am–5pm. Parking $3.

Movieland Wax Museum   Visit with the stars—or just amazingly lifelike replicas! For over 30 years this touristy yet compelling attraction has been documenting movie history in their own slightly warped way, by adding wax celebrities to their collection of over 275 figures. Classic stars such as Julie Andrews, John Wayne, and Bette Davis bring back memories of the silver screen, while current celebs like Leonardo DiCaprio, Julia Roberts, and Jack Nicholson keep 'em up-to-date.

7711 Beach Blvd., Buena Park. ☎ **714/522-1155.** Fax 714/739-9668. www. movielandwaxmuseum.com. Admission $12.95 adults, $10.55 seniors 55+, $6.95 children 4–11, 3 and under free. Mon–Fri 10am–7:30pm; Sat–Sun 9am-8:30pm.

Orange County Museum of Art   Located near Newport Beach's Fashion Island, this museum houses a 6,500-piece collection chronicling California's unique art history from the mid-19th century to the present. Distinctive traveling exhibits from museums around the globe complement OCMA's permanent collection and provide an international context for interpreting the art of California.

850 San Clemente Dr., Newport Beach. ☎ **949/759-1122.** Fax 949/759-5623. www.ocma.net. Admission $5 adults, $4 seniors and students, free to kids under 16. Tue–Sun 11am–5pm.

Richard Nixon Library and Birthplace *₢*   Although he was the most vilified U.S. president in modern history, there has always been a warm place in the hearts of Orange County locals for Richard Nixon. This presidential library, located in Nixon's boyhood town, celebrates the roots, life, and legacy of America's 37th President. The 9-acre site contains the modest farmhouse where Nixon was born, manicured flower gardens, a modern museum housing presidential archives, and the final resting place of Mr. Nixon and his wife, Pat.

Displays include videos of the famous Nixon-Kennedy TV debates, an impressive life-size statuary summit of world leaders, gifts of state (including a gun from Elvis), and exhibits on China and Russia. There's also a display of Pat Nixon's First Lady gowns and a 12-foot-high graffiti-covered chunk of the Berlin Wall, symbolizing the defeat of Communism, but hardly a mention is made of Nixon's role in the anti-Communist witch-hunts of the 1950s. Similarly, there are exhibits on Vietnam, yet no mention of Nixon's illegal expansion of that war into neighboring Cambodia.

Only the Watergate Gallery is relatively forthright, allowing visitors to listen to actual White House tapes and view a montage of the president's last day in the White House.

18001 Yorba Linda Blvd., Yorba Linda. 🅒 **714/993-5075**. Fax 714/993-3393. www. nixonlibrary.org. Admission $5.95 adults, $3.95 seniors, $2 children 8–11, free for children 7 and under. Mon–Sat 10am–5pm; Sun 11am–5pm.

NEARBY SHOPPING

The Block at Orange   At the intersection of hip and hipper, this outdoor urban streetscape mall features over 100 distinctive shops, restaurants, and entertainment venues that cater to the young and trendy with disposable income. Specialty retail stores include Hilo Hattie—the Store of Hawaii, Ron John Surf Shop, MARS Music, and Borders Books & Music. After shopping, entertainment ranges from GameWorks or Vans Skate Park to Burke Williams Day Spa and a 30-screen AMC Theater. 1 City Blvd., Orange. 🅒 **877/2-THE-BLOCK** or 714/769-4000. www.blockatorange.com.

City of Orange Antique District   You can tell just by looking at downtown Orange's old-fashioned bandstand and central plaza (think *The Music Man*) that this is a great place for antiquing. The two main streets that intersect at the heart of town are Chapman and Glassell streets; both are lined with vintage commercial buildings now used as multi-vendor antique malls, where each seller creates a cozy little setting to suit their particular collectibles.

Fashion Island Newport Beach   It's actually *not* an island, unless you count the nearly impenetrable sea of skyscrapers that border this posh mall, which is designed to resemble an open-air Mediterranean village. Anchored by Neiman Marcus, Bloomingdale's, and Macy's, the mall is lined with outdoor artwork, upscale shops, and specialty boutiques including Allen Allen women's casual wear and the trendy Optical Shop of Aspen; 12 different restaurants offer something for everyone. 401 Newport Center Dr., Newport Beach. 🅒 **949/721-2000**. www.fashionisland-nb.com.

South Coast Plaza   South Coast Plaza, one of the most upscale shopping complexes in the world, is so big, it's a day's adventure itself. It's home to some of fashion's most prominent boutiques, including Emporio Armani, Chanel, Alfred Dunhill, and Coach; beautiful branches of the nation's top department stores such as Saks Fifth Avenue and Nordstrom; and outposts of high-end specialty shops like Williams Sonoma, L.A. Eyeworks, and Rizzoli Booksellers. The mall is also home to many impressive works of modern art, and snacking and dining options are a cut above as well—you won't find Hot-Dog-on-a-Stick among the 40 or so restaurants. Wolfgang Puck Cafe, Morton's of Chicago, Ghirardelli Soda Fountain, Planet Hollywood, and Scott's Seafood Grill lure the hungry away from Del Taco and McDonald's. 3333 Bristol St. (at I-405), Costa Mesa. ✆ 800/782-8888 or 714/435-2000. www.southcoastplaza.com.

7

After Dark Entertainment & Nightlife

We congratulate anyone who, after a day spent touring the theme parks, has energy left over for nighttime adventures—in this chapter you'll find a rundown of clubs, performing arts venues, and spectator sports options both in and out of the Disneyland Resort.

If you'd like to peruse listings for live performances and cultural events in the Orange County area, pick up a copy of the *O.C. Weekly* (www.ocweekly.com), a free alternative newspaper with comprehensive arts and entertainment listings; the *Los Angeles Times* Sunday "Calendar" and Thursday "Weekend" sections (online at www.calendarlive.com) also feature listings throughout L.A. and Orange counties. Music fans can log onto **www.localmusic.com**, which provides 2 weeks' worth of show schedules conveniently organized by neighborhood and/or style; or try **www.gigmania. com**, where you can search by date, club, or artist, and access links to music clips and online CD stores.

1 In the Disneyland Resort

When the **Downtown Disney** entertainment district—sort of a Disneyfied version of the successful Universal CityWalk in Los Angeles—opened in 2001, it filled a void that had existed for years at Disneyland: What do grownups do for fun after the park closes (or when we have had enough Mickey for one day)? Finally, there are some bona fide after dark choices that eliminate the need to leave the Disneyland Resort—which was the planners' intention all along!

The Mississippi delta–flavored **House of Blues** (© 714/778-**BLUE;** www.hob.com) is a funky, midsize (900 people) venue that features blues, rock 'n' roll, and country performers as varied as Merle Haggard, Dogstar, George Thorogood, and Duran Duran. Drawing an audience from throughout the Southland, HOB transcends its theme park-adjacent location and is a bona fide player venue on the national music scene. For information on the House of Blues restaurant, see p. 73.

Every night, a rowdy jazz ensemble plays at the French Quarter-style **Ralph Brennan's Jazz Kitchen** (© 714/776-5200; www.rbjazzkitchen.com), where the dual legacies of New Orleans—food and music—are served up in a whimsical setting depicting the Big Easy's charm, ambiance and hospitality (also see the restaurant listing on p. 74). Each evening sends waves of Southern-style tunes out into the Downtown Disney esplanade.

Spicy Latin music sets the stage at Miami-grown **Y Arriba Y Arriba** (© 714/533-8272; www.yarribayarriba.com), whose *teatro* (theater) features live entertainment ranging from an in-house dance orchestra to specialty acts and concerts by big-name Latin guest stars. For information on the Y Arriba Y Arriba restaurant, see p. 76.

Sports fans will be happy to see an outpost of the Disney-owned **ESPN Zone,** 1545 Disneyland Dr. (© 714/300-ESPN; www.espnzone.com), where sporting events are broadcast throughout the dining rooms and indoor/outdoor bar, creating a loud, arena-style atmosphere that's the perfect backdrop for crowd-pleasing American grill food and pub favorites. Radio and television sports programs (including ESPN's *Up Close*) broadcast live from the complex, and the interactive "Sports Arena" offers virtual and actual competitive games, including a 30-foot rock-climbing wall.

If you use vacation time to get around to seeing movies, you'll be happy to find a spiffy new **AMC Theatres** (© 714/769-4262) 12-screen multiplex right next to the Disneyland Hotel. Offering stadium seating and state-of-the-art sound, AMC is a convenient option and is usually running the latest major releases.

2 In Orange County

PERFORMING ARTS

CONCERT HALLS & AUDITORIUMS　　The **Arrowhead Pond of Anaheim,** 2695 E. Katella Ave., Anaheim (© 714/704-2400; www.arrowheadpond.com) is one of Southern California's main venues for a variety of sports and entertainment. The Pond is home to the NHL Mighty Ducks of Anaheim (see "Spectator Sports," below) and hosts a variety of premier family shows, top-billed concerts, popular sports and entertainment events throughout the year. The 19,200-seat facility is located on the corner of Katella Ave. and Douglass Road, a short drive from the Disneyland Resort.

Tips After Dark in the Parks

When darkness falls in Disneyland and California Adventure, each park presents special performances that project into the night sky. Schedules for all shows and parades vary each day according to the season and park hours, but the timetable is available months in advance by calling Disney or checking the website (see chapter 2, "Planning Your Trip to the Disneyland Resort" and chapter 6, "What to See and Do at the Disneyland Resort," for contact information).

• There's always been a parade through the flower-lined paths of Disneyland's central hub and Fantasyland; for 26 years it was the Main Street Electrical Parade (which now appears at California Adventure, see below), and features a new production every few years, with different themes, costumes, and floats. The parade is one of Disneyland's most popular events, and people stake out spots along the route an hour or more before show time; the fireworks usually follow the last parade of the night. At press time, the featured theme was **"Parade of the Stars,"** conjured to celebrate Disneyland's 45th anniversary (in 2000) with a nostalgic look back at classic Disney characters and new favorites; cast members interact with viewers, and themed music blares along with each colorful float.

• **Believe, There's Magic in the Stars** is Disneyland's official name for the nightly fireworks show above Sleeping Beauty's Castle, a 10-minute display of the latest pyrotechnics accompanied by amplified music—and plenty of "ooohs" and "aaahs" from the audience. The lightshow ends with a bang—and with the traditional descent of Tinkerbell to the castle ramparts. (Between Thanksgiving and New Years, the holiday version of the show features red and green firework effects and a snow-filled finale—but no Tinkerbell). Optimal viewing spots are directly in front of the Castle and at the end of Main Street U.S.A., but be prepared for shoulder-crushing crowds, especially during periods of peak visitation.

• Performed on a stage that rises from the harbor at New Orleans Square, **Fantasmic!** is a laser, firework, and projection special effects extravaganza that features Mickey

Mouse in his *Fantasia* "sorcerer's apprentice" persona, encountering good, evil, and all your favorite Disney characters along the way. The show features filmed sequences projected onto screens of water, live performances, laser light shows, fireworks, and fog effects—it's loud and bright, and small children who are easily frightened shouldn't sit too close. It's worth noting that fans begin staking out prime viewing spots between 1-2 hours before show time, often spreading blankets to reserve space for their entire group so some can continue touring the park while others hold their chosen space. *Tip:* A Fantasmic! Dessert Buffet is offered for each performance; for $41 a person you can enjoy all-you-can-eat dessert and seating on the Disney Gallery balcony directly across from the stage. Reservations must be made (as early in the day as possible) at the Guest Relations window near the main entrance for this splurge.

- Shortly after its opening, California Adventure announced the return of the **Electrical Parade**, which winds nightly through the park. Originally called the "Main Street Electrical Parade," the bulb-festooned floats glided and twirled their way to Disney's Florida park for a while, before returning to Anaheim in 2001. Even in the day and age of high-tech, people still thrill to the spectacle of hundreds of illuminated light bulbs glowing in unison.

- **Eureka!** at California Adventure, offers an upbeat, colorful celebration of the Golden State. It's a departure from the typical Disney presentation, and features groups of high-energy performers parading in flamboyant costumes (think Mardi Gras meets Las Vegas) to represent California's cultural heritage, recreational pursuits, and physical landscape. Many floats are action-packed, bearing skateboarders, trapeze-artist drummers, tumbling acrobats, and wackiness like Chinese take-out food on stilts (watch the chow mein chase the fortune cookie!). The music is contemporary and catchy, but the floats often make reference to California locales or features than can be lost on out-of-staters.

One of the largest musical theater companies in Southern California, the award-winning **Fullerton Civic Light Opera,** 218 W. Commonwealth Ave., Fullerton (© **714/879-1732;** www.fclo.com) produces four professional Broadway-style musicals in a season that runs from February through November. Ten minutes from the Disneyland Resort, the theater is in Fullerton, a quiet community with a quaint, historic downtown. Ticket prices range from $16-$38.

The **Orange County Performing Arts Center,** 600 Town Center Dr., Costa Mesa (© 714/556-2121; www.ocpac.org) is renowned for its asymmetrical architecture, advanced acoustical design and excellent sightlines. The 3,000-seat Segerstrom Hall hosts a full season of the latest touring Broadway productions as well as an international classic dance season. The 300-seat Founders Hall offers jazz and cabaret programming as well as chamber music. The Center is also home to the Philharmonic Society of Orange County, Pacific Symphony Orchestra, Opera Pacific, the William Hall Master Chorale and Pacific Chorale.

The intimate **Sun Theatre,** 2200 E. Katella Ave., Anaheim (© **714/712-2700;** www.sun-theatre.com) brings headliners like Styx, Yes, George Benson, REO Speedwagon, Dwight Yoakam, and Brian Wilson up close and personal. No seat is more than 80 feet from the stage, and an acclaimed dinner menu is served in selected sections. Prices vary with each performer and event.

THEATER **South Coast Repertory,** 655 Town Center Dr., Costa Mesa (© **714/708-5500;** www.scr.org) is about 25 minutes away from the Disneyland Resort. Boasting almost 40 seasons of presenting live professional theater in southern California, the Tony award-winning South Coast Repertory showcases six classic productions on the main stage and five contemporary productions on the intimate second stage each season. SCR also presents two holiday productions annually. Tickets range in price from $23 to $52.

SPECTATOR SPORTS

While local sports fans bemoan Southern California's lack of an NFL football team, there are plenty of high-energy games to occupy your time in the Orange County area—and all the way up to L.A.'s $300 million, state-of-the-art STAPLES Center.

BASEBALL The Disney-owned **Anaheim Angels** (© **714/634-2000** for information, 714/663-9000 to order tickets; www.

angelsbaseball.com) play at the 45,000-seat Edison Field, 2000 Gene Autry Way (near Katella Avenue), in Anaheim. The season runs from April through October; tickets range in price from $7 to $35, with the average decent seat costing about $10 to $15.

The **Los Angeles Dodgers** (℗ 213/224-1500) play at Dodger Stadium, 1000 Elysian Park, near Sunset Boulevard. The team's slick, interactive website (www.dodgers.com) offers everything from game schedules to souvenir merchandise online.

BASKETBALL   Los Angeles has two NBA franchises: the **L.A. Lakers** (℗ 800/LAKERS-LA or 310/419-3100; www.lakers.com), hot off their 2000 and 2001 NBA Championships and basking in the talent of superstars Shaquille O'Neal and Kobe Bryant; and the **L.A. Clippers** (℗ 213/745-0400; www.clippers.com), a former San Diego team (in L.A. since 1984) who plays well but is always overshadowed by the Laker machine. Both teams play in the **STAPLES Center** in downtown L.A., 1111 S. Figueroa St. (℗ 877/673-6799; www.staplescenterla.com). Lakers tickets range in price from $21 to $160, but can be hard to come by (especially when celebrity fans like Jack Nicholson and Dyan Cannon nab the best seats), so try to plan ahead. Tickets to see the Clippers are usually in the $10 to $100 range, and are generally more easily purchased closer to game day.

The WNBA's **L.A. Sparks** (℗ 310/330-2434; www.lasparks.com) also play at the STAPLES Center in a season that runs from late May to August; winners of the 2001 WNBA championship, the Sparks are especially proud of star center (and Olympic gold medalist) Lisa Leslie.

FOOTBALL   Though lacking an NFL team, Southern California football fans are blessed with two popular college teams. The college ball season runs from September to November; if you're interested in checking out a game, contact **UCLA Bruins Football** (℗ 310/825-2106; www.uclabruins.fansonly.com) or **USC Trojans Football** (℗ 213/740-2311; www.usctrojans.com).

New to the region is the arena football team **Los Angeles Avengers** (℗ 310/473-7999; www.laavengers.com), who play at the STAPLES Center. Led by former LA Raiders quarterback Todd Marinovich, the team also draws fans for their Avenger cheerleaders, known as the A-Team.

HOCKEY   The **Mighty Ducks of Anaheim** (℗ 714/940-2159; www.mightyducks.com) are a Disney-owned NHL franchise, backed by top scorers Paul Kariya and Teemu Selanne and the impressive goalkeeping skills of Guy Hebert. They play between September and April at the Arrowhead Pond of Anaheim (2695 E. Katella Ave.) a short drive from the Disneyland Resort; ticket prices range from $15 to $75.

The NHL's **L.A. Kings** (*©* **310/673-6003;** www.lakings.com), also call the STAPLES Center home.

8

Other Southern California Family Attractions

While the Disneyland Resort is the recognized frontrunner in family-friendly vacation destinations in Southern California, there are other appealing options for day trips or quick overnight excursions—and a terrific way to experience even more of the Golden State.

1 Knott's Berry Farm

ESSENTIALS

GETTING THERE

Knott's Berry Farm is at 8039 Beach Blvd. in Buena Park. It's about a 10-minute ride north on I-5 from Disneyland. From I-5 or Calif. 91, exit south onto Beach Boulevard. The park is about half a mile south of Calif. 91.

VISITOR INFORMATION

The **Buena Park Convention and Visitors Office,** 6280 Manchester Blvd., Suite 103 (© **800/541-3953** or 714/562-3560; www.buenapark.com/cvo), provides specialized information on the area, including Knott's Berry Farm.

To learn more about the amusement park before you arrive, call © **714/220-5200** or log onto **www.knotts.com**.

ADMISSION PRICES & OPERATING HOURS

Admission to the park, including unlimited access to all rides, shows, and attractions, is $40 for adults and children 12 and over, $30 for seniors 60 or better, kids 3 to 11, non-ambulatory visitors, and expectant mothers; children under 3 are admitted free. Admission after 4pm (on any day the park is open past 6pm) is $20 for adults and $15 for kids 3 to 11. Parking is $7. Tickets can also be purchased at many Southern California hotels, where discount coupons are sometimes available.

Like Disneyland, Knott's offers discounted admission for Southern California residents during the off-season, so if you're bringing local friends or family members along, try to take advantage of the bargain. Also like Disneyland, Knott's Berry Farm's hours vary from week to week so call ahead. The park generally is open during the summer daily from 9am to midnight. The rest of the year, it opens at 10am and closes at 6 or 8pm, except Saturday, when it stays open until 10pm. Knott's is closed December 25. Special hours and prices are in effect during Knott's Scary Farm in late October. Stage shows and special activities are scheduled throughout the day. Pick up a schedule at the ticket booth.

GUEST SERVICES

Lockers   Lockers are available outside the Grand Entrance, at Wild Water Wilderness, and at the Ghost Town locker facility; fees range from $1 to $3.

Strollers and Wheelchairs   Strollers and wheelchairs are available inside the Grand Entrance adjacent to the Snoopy fountain; strollers rent for $7-$10 a day, wheelchairs for $7 (refundable security deposits are required). Electric wheelchairs, which must be reserved in advance, rent for $30 a day.

Lost Child Center   Any child appearing to be lost will be taken to the Lost Child Center in Calico Square; parents should locate the Center on a map, and advise kids to find a costumed park employee in the event they become separated from the group.

Baby-Changing and Nursing Stations   You'll find baby care convenience stations in the California MarketPlace, Camp Snoopy, and Wild Water Wilderness.

First Aid   There is a First Aid Center in Ghost Town. Nurses are on duty during park operating hours.

Guests With Special Needs   Knott's has created a *Rider Safety Guide* that provides information on wheelchair and non-ambulatory guest access to rides and attractions. Pick one up at the ticket booth when you arrive—you may also request one in advance by calling Guest Services (© **714/220-5220**).

TOURING THE PARK

Knott's Berry Farm maintains much of its original Old West motif, but also features the "Peanuts" gang: Snoopy, Charlie Brown, Woodstock, and pals are the official costumed characters of Knott's. The park is divided into six themed areas, each one of which features at least one of the thrill roller coasters that are Knotts's claim to fame. The California MarketPlace is located adjacent to, but outside of the theme park, featuring 14 unique shops and restaurants including the original favorite, Mrs. Knott's Chicken Dinner Restaurant.

GHOST TOWN

The park's original attraction is a collection of 19th-century buildings relocated from deserted Old West towns. You can pan for gold, ride the Butterfield Stagecoach, take rickety train cars through the Calico Mine, watch cowboys shoot it out on the wooden sidewalks of town, and enjoy frontier-style entertainment in the Calico Saloon.

Ghost Town Artisans 😊 *(Finds* A delightful holdover from the earliest days of the park, these living history booths present old-time crafts and tall tales presented by costumed blacksmiths, woodcarvers, a spinner, and storytellers who help bring Ghost Town to life for curious kids and history buffs.

Ghost Town Calico Railroad Board this narrow-gauge steam-powered train for a fun round-trip tour of the park, interrupted by "bandit" holdups.

GhostRider 😊😊😊 Looming 118 feet high, this coaster is the single largest attraction in park history and one of the longest and tallest wooden roller coasters in the world. Riders enter through a replica mine, and are strapped into gold, silver, and copper mining cars for an adventure that twists and careens through sudden dips, banked turns, and cheek-flattening G-forces.

Timber Mountain Log Ride 😊😊 Everyone gets a good soaking on this high-speed log ride, where riders emerge from a dark and twisting waterway and plummet down a flume for the grand splash.

Wild West Stunt Show This wild and woolly stunt spectacular is a raucous salute to the Old West presented throughout the day in the open air Wagon Camp Theater.

GHOST TOWN SHOPPING

Western-themed stores offer souvenirs that range from western apparel and leather goods to hand-dipped candles and other crafts from the artisan displays.

FIESTA VILLAGE

Here you'll find a south-of-the-border theme. That means festive markets and an ambiance that suggests old Spanish California.

A cluster of carnival-style rides (in addition to the roller coasters listed below) includes a 100-year-old merry-go-round, plus Knott's version of Disneyland's Tea Cups, where you can sit-and-spin your own sombrero. Mariachi bands stroll the paths of Fiesta Village, which are lined with old-time carnival games and state-of-the-art electric arcades. In a quieter lakeside setting, there's a steepled Church of Reflection; hundreds of couples tie the knot here each year.

Electric Nights Edison International co-sponsors this night-time spectacular blending pyrotechnics, lasers, water and light effects with a stirring score of pop, American, and "Peanuts" musical favorites.

Jaguar! Loosely themed around a tropical jungle setting, this wild roller coaster includes two heart-in-the-mouth drops and a loop that turns you upside down.

Montezooma's Revenge Blasting from 0 to 60mph in 3 seconds, this not-for-the-fainthearted thriller then propels riders through *two* giant 360° loops.

SHOPPING IN FIESTA VILLAGE

Spanish-style arches frame **Casa California,** the park's largest selection of logo merchandise, Snoopy souvenir items and gifts.

THE BOARDWALK

The park's most recently added area is a salute to Southern California's beach culture, where colorful architecture and palm trees are the backdrop for a trio of thrill rides. Other amusements include arcade and boardwalk games, the **Dinosaur Discover Center,** and the **Charles M. Schulz Theatre,** where seasonal productions include a SNOOPY ice show or holiday pageant (check the marquee or park entertainment schedule for showtimes).

Boomerang This corkscrew scream machine sends you twisting through six head-over-heels loops in less than a minute—but it doesn't end there, since you're sent through the track again . . . backwards!

Lazer Invaders *(Kids* In this adaptation of the classic "Lazer Runner," participants equipped with phasers and fiber optic vests battle for supremacy in a richly evocative atmosphere. Each combatant must make use of protective walls and laser power to vanquish opponents.

Kingdom of the Dinosaurs Go back in time with this attraction featuring extremely realistic *Jurassic Park*-like creatures.

Perilous Plunge ⚘⚘⚘   Just 34 feet shorter than Niagara Falls, this wet adventure sends riders to a height of 127 feet and then drops them down a 115-foot water chute at a 75° angle—15 degrees from a sheer vertical. Prepare for a thorough soaking (a boon on hot days, but best experienced before dark all other times).

Sky Cabin ⚘   Just when you were thinking all the rides were for hardcore adrenaline-seekers (most are, actually), this quiet ride offers the same spectacular views at a calmer pace. The slowly rotating "cabin" ascends Knott's vertical tower, providing panoramic views of the park and surrounding area.

Supreme Scream ⚘⚘   They could've called this one the "Broken Elevator"—riders are propelled straight up a 254-foot tower in mere seconds, then plunged downward at more than 50 miles per hour. The whole descent only takes a terrifying 3 seconds.

BOARDWALK SHOPPING

Over a dozen vendor carts and retail shops provide signature clothing, hats, and souvenirs; surf-themed sun items; sweet treats at the Candy Cottage; an array of Peanuts souvenirs; prehistoric toys at Dinostore Digs; and trendy styles for young girls at Girl Power.

CAMP SNOOPY *(Kids*

This will probably be the youngsters' favorite area. It's meant to recreate a wilderness camp in the High Sierras, whose six rustic acres are the playgrounds of Charles Schulz's beagle and his pals, Charlie Brown and Lucy, who greet guests and pose for pictures. There are over a dozen rides in the Camp; several kid-sized rides are made especially for the younger set, while the entire family can enjoy others. Scaled down stock cars, locomotives, steamboats, 18-wheeler semis, hot-air balloons, and even the Peanuts gang's school bus give kids a playland of their own; there's even a child-sized version of Supreme Scream, called Woodstock's Airmail. Interactive attractions include a petting zoo, walk-through Camp Headquarters, and hands-on Inventors Workshop.

WILD WATER WILDERNESS

This $10 million, 3½-acre area is styled like a turn-of-the-century California wilderness park with a raging white water river, cascading waterfalls, soaring geysers, and old-style ranger stations.

Bigfoot Rapids ⚘⚘⚘   The centerpiece of Wild Water Wilderness is this outdoor whitewater river raft ride, the longest of its kind in the world. Climb aboard a six-seat circular raft, and prepare to be

---

Tips **Getting Soaked at Knott's**

Surf's up at **Knott's Soak City U.S.A.,** a new 13-acre water park next door to Knott's Berry Farm. Water thrill-seekers of all ages can get soaked on 21 water rides and attractions, to the theme of surf woodies and longboards of the 1950s Southern California coast. The fun includes tube and body slides, speed slides, an artificial wave lagoon, and an area for youngsters with their own pool and beach shack fun house. The park is located at 8039, Buena Park (© **714/220-5200;** www.soakcityusa.com), and admission prices are $21.95 for adults, $14.95 for kids 3 to 11, and free to children under 3; parking is $7. Ask about special promotions and discount coupons (or check the website). The park is open weekends in April, May, and September, then daily between Memorial Day and Labor Day. Soak City U.S.A. opens at 10am and closes between 6 and 8pm, based on the season.

---

bounced, buffeted, tossed, spun, and splashed along fast moving currents, under cascading waterfalls, and around soaring geysers. Let there be no doubt: you will get *extremely* wet on this one.

Mystery Lodge 🎔🎔 This amazing high-tech, trick-of-the-eye tribute to the magic of Native American storytelling is a theater attraction for the whole family. The "Old Storyteller" takes the audience on a mystical, multi-sensory journey into the culture of local tribes by employing centuries-old legends passed down through oral history.

SHOPPING IN WILD WATER WILDERNESS

If getting soaked by Bigfoot Rapids isn't enough, the ill-prepared can also get soaked at **Bigfoot Exporters,** who conveniently carry towels and dry clothing. On the other hand, there's the **Mystery Lodge Store,** which features Native-made gifts from the Pacific Northwest Coast, specializing in authentic totems, bentwood boxes, tribal masks, carvings, and jewelry, all handcrafted by Native Americans.

INDIAN TRAILS

Explore the ride-free Indian Trails cultural area, which offers daily demonstrations of native dance and music by authentically costumed Native American and Aztec dancers, singers and musicians performed in the round on the Indian Trails stage. In addition, the compound showcases a variety of traditional Native American structures from the Pacific Northwest, Great Plains, and Southwest. The area includes four towering totem poles, standing from 15 to 27 feet high; three authentic tipis, representing the Arapaho, Blackfoot, and Nez Perce tribes; and more. The Arts and Crafts of Native American tribes from the western part of North America are also demonstrated and displayed. While exploring Indian Trails, visitors can enjoy a sampling of Native American foods, including Navajo tacos, Indian fry bread, and fresh roasted ears of corn.

WHERE TO STAY & DINE

Since Knott's Berry Farm and Disneyland are nearby neighbors, most of the Anaheim hotels listed in chapter 4, "Accommodations," are ideally located for visiting the park; the closest one is the Radisson Resort Knott's Berry Farm, which you'll find in the "Elsewhere in Orange County" section.

You'll find almost two dozen dining choices in the park, the best of which is Mrs. Knott's Chicken Dinner Restaurant (see p. 78 for a full listing). For choices outside Knott's Berry Farm, please refer to chapter 5, "Dining."

2 Universal Studios Hollywood

ESSENTIALS

GETTING THERE

Universal Studios Hollywood is located in Universal City, between Hollywood and the San Fernando Valley. Take the U.S. 101 Freeway to either Lankershim Boulevard or Universal Center Drive and follow the signs to parking for Universal Studios and Universal CityWalk.

Visitors based in the Anaheim area can take the Universal Express Bus from the AirportBus Transportation Center located at 1415 Manchester Avenue near Disneyland (hotel pickup is also available at no extra charge). The ride is complimentary, but Universal tickets must be purchased in advance by calling 1-800-UNIVERSAL; be sure to reserve room on the Express Bus when you call. The shuttle runs four times a day in each direction, with extended service during the peak summer months.

VISITOR INFORMATION

For Universal Studios Hollywood information, call © 818/662-3801 or log onto www.universalstudioshollywood.com.

For general Los Angeles-area information, contact the **Los Angeles Convention & Visitors Bureau** (© **800/366-6116;** Events Hotline 213/689-8822; www.lacvb.com).

ADMISSION PRICES & OPERATING HOURS

Admission to the park, including all rides, attractions, and live shows, is $43 for adults, $37 for seniors 60 and better, $33 for kids 3 to 11, and free for children under 3. Parking is $7. Universal is open daily from 9am; closing hours vary according to season and day of the week (usually 6–10pm). The park also offers several other admission plans, including multi-day and season passes, and a "Director's Pass," with front-of-the-line privileges; group VIP passes (essentially private tours); and passes which are good for admission to other Southern California attractions, including Seaworld San Diego. Call ahead for specific information for your visit. *Note:* The park is subject to closure on Thanksgiving and Christmas, so check ahead before planning a holiday trip.

GUEST SERVICES

You'll find a Guest Relations booth near the main gate; there's one both outside and just inside the entrance. In addition to those listed below, services include complimentary kennel facilities, lost children's center, ATM machines, lost and found, and coin-operated lockers.

Stroller and Wheelchair Rental   Rentals are located in the Upper Lot. Stroller check-ins are located in two convenient spots; at the Backlot Tram Tour and in the Lower Lot near the base of the Starway. The daily rental fee for strollers or wheelchairs is $5.

Guests with Disabilities   Universal leads the theme park pack in providing complete and convenient access for disabled guests. Every ride, show, attraction, escalator, and parking structure is designed to accommodate guests in a wheelchair or guests with other disabilities. There are designated disabled guest entrances for all attractions in the park. You can pick up Universal's official detailed guide for guests with disabilities at Guest Relations (see above).

TOURING THE PARK

Believing that filmmaking itself was a bona fide attraction; Universal Studios began offering tours in 1964. The concept worked. Today Universal is more than just one of the largest movie studios in the world—it's one of the biggest amusement parks. Universal Studios is a really fun place. But just as in any theme park, lines can be long; the wait for a 5-minute ride can sometimes last

ACCOMMODATIONS

Best Western Mikado Hotel **4**

Beverly Garland's Holiday Inn **4**

Hilton Universal City & Towers **2**

Radisson Valley Center **4**

Safari Inn **1**

Sheraton Universal Hotel **3**

Sportsmen's Lodge **4**

more than an hour. In summer, the stifling Valley heat can dog you all day. To avoid the crowds, skip weekends, school vacations, and Japanese holidays.

RIDES & ATTRACTIONS

Back to the Future *☆☆☆* Popular since it first opened, this virtual-reality ride is one of the park's most popular, despite constant competition from newer attractions. In this simulation chamber (like Star Tours at Disneyland), you're seated in a time-traveling DeLorean and thrust into a multimedia roller-coasting extravaganza.

Backlot Tour *☆☆☆* Don't miss this 1-hour guided tram ride around the company's 420 acres. En route, you pass stars' dressing rooms and production offices before visiting famous back-lot sets that include an eerily familiar Old West town, a New York City street, and the town square from the *Back to the Future* films. Along the way the tram encounters several staged "disasters," which we won't divulge here lest we ruin the surprise.

E.T. Adventure Hop aboard a spacebike with the beloved extra-terrestrial; you can feel the wind in your face as you swoop through the universe trying to save E.T. and his dying home planet. Every rider is successful of course, as this all ages (42" and above only) ride attempts to recreate the wonder of the cinema version.

Jurassic Park III—Summer Splash 🦖🦖   Reworked in 2001 to coincide with the third *Jurassic Park* release, this special-effects showcase is short in duration but long on dinosaur illusions and computer magic. The technical advancements of this interactive ride are impressive, as riders in jungle boats enter a 3-dimensional world of five-story-tall T-rexes and airborne raptors that culminates in a pitch-dark vertical drop with a splash ending.

LUCY—A Tribute   An exhibit honoring the Queen of Comedy, Lucille Ball, with personal memorabilia, as well as items related to her long television career, including some of her Emmys, and letters from famous fans. There is also behind-the-scenes and personal footage of Ball, Desi Arnaz, and their family.

The Mummy Returns: Chamber of Doom 🦖   Based on the Universal film still in theaters when this attraction opened, the park's most recent addition is a series of realistic walk-through movie sets arranged as a maze, where visitors wander from a creepy Ancient Egyptian tomb complete with weathered hieroglyphics and dusty cobwebs through galleries of props from the production.

Nickelodeon Blast Zone 🦖🦖 *Kids*   For the under-42" crowd left out of the main event thrill rides, this self-contained park-within-a-park has a host of rides and attractions featuring characters and themes from the kids-only TV network: There's a *Rugrats* magic show, the *Wild Thornberry's* rough-and-tumble play area, a water play area, and even a Nick Jr. playground for the smallest visitors.

Terminator 2: 3-D 🦖🦖🦖   This high-tech virtual adventure utilizes triple-screen technology to impact all the senses with explosions and laser fire coming from all sides. This cyber-war was created with the help of James Cameron, director of the *Terminator* movie series.

The World of Cinemagic 🦖   Take a rare look behind the scenes at how special effects are created in the movies. Three separate sound stages highlight "The Magic of Alfred Hitchcock," "*Back to the Future* Special Effects," and "Nutty Professor Sound Effects Show." Volunteers from the audience recreate movie special effects against a special blue screen, or help mix sound into a silent strip of film.

LIVE SHOWS

Animal Planet Live!   Teaming up with cable's Animal Planet channel, Universal brings their most popular shows to life in this humorous, interactive experience. Combining live animals from pigs to hawks with video segments on a giant screen, the show brings to life moments from *Animal Planet Sports, Emergency Vets, Wild on the Set, Planet's Funniest Animals,* and *The Jeff Corwin Experience.* Animal Planet Live! also integrates demonstrations by clever animal stars, multimedia effects, human costars, and sketches into a lively family entertainment.

Backdraft ✹✹ Based on the Ron Howard movie *Backdraft,* this five-alarm special effects thriller recreates the film's scorching warehouse scene; although the audience stands amidst realistic ruptured fuel lines and melting metal—and the blaze is real, live flames—you'll barely break a sweat (except from the suspense, that is!).

WaterWorld ✹ The Kevin Costner flick may have been a box-office snore, but the live action stunt show based on the film is thrilling, with jet skiers who slingshot into the air from submerged catapults, a seaplane that crashes in an explosion of fireballs, and gallons of water that surge beneath breathtaking pyrotechnics.

The Wild, Wild, Wild West Stunt Show There's always been a stunt show at Universal, and it seems like they improve on it each season. The latest is a daring display of film history's memorable and dangerous screen feats that unfold in a 15-minute extravaganza of high plank falls, shattering buildings, whirlwind gun- and fistfights, horseplay, and explosions. It's an action comedy, though, with enough humor to keep younger viewers from getting too scared.

UNIVERSAL CITYWALK

Designed to resemble an almost-cartoonish depiction of an urban street, Universal CityWalk is unique. Situated next door to Universal Studios—in fact, you must walk through it if you use Universal City's main parking structure—CityWalk is dominated by brightly colored, oversize storefronts. Expanded in recent years to include a restaurant-dominated wing with larger-than-life video screens and a sound system that bombards the senses day and night, CityWalk teems with restless youth on the weekends. The heavily touristed faux street is home to over 25 restaurants, cafes, and fast-food stands; highlights include **B.B. King's Blues Club,** the newest **Hard Rock Cafe,** a branch of the **Hollywood Athletic Club** featuring a restaurant and pool hall, raucous family-style Buca di Beppo Italian restaurant, and rock 'n' roll sushi at Wasabi. It's an enclosed entertainment zone without cruising cars or sensitive neighbors. With a noisy, carnival atmosphere, CityWalk is almost an amusement park in its own right, and a favorite escape for locals.

CityWalk's diverse retail ranges from youthquake essentials like Skechers, Quiksilver Boardrider's Club, Fossil, and Sam Goody Superstore to more esoteric fare at All Star Collectibles, Wound & Wound Toy Company, Upstart Crow Bookstore, and the Universal Studio Store. There's even a UCLA logo-wear boutique and fine arts at Martin Lawrence Museum Shop.

WHERE TO STAY & DINE

Since Universal City is in L.A.'s San Fernando Valley, most of the Los Angeles-area hotels listed in chapter 4, "Accommodations," are ideally located for visiting the park; the closest ones are the Hilton Universal City and the Sheraton Universal, which are just a short walk or shuttle ride from the park. You'll find full listings for both in the "Near Universal Studios" section.

There are over 35 dining choices at the park, including those in Universal CityWalk (see above). For choices outside Universal Studios Hollywood, please refer to chapter 5, "Dining."

3 LEGOLAND

ESSENTIALS
GETTING THERE

LEGOLAND is located at 1 Lego Drive in Carlsbad, a seaside town approximately 1 hour from Anaheim and 30 minutes from downtown San Diego. From I-5 take the Cannon Rd. exit east, following signs for Lego Drive.

VISITOR INFORMATION

For information on LEGOLAND, call © **877/534-6526** or 760/918-LEGO; you can also find out everything about the park—and take a virtual tour—online at **www.legolandca.com**.

If you'd like to learn more about the surrounding area, the **Carlsbad Visitor Information Center,** 400 Carlsbad Village Dr. (in the old Santa Fe Depot) (© **800/227-5722** or 760/434-6093; www.carlsbadca.org), has lots of additional information on beaches and Carlsbad's famous flower fields.

ADMISSION PRICES & OPERATING HOURS

Admission to LEGOLAND is $38 for adults, $32 for seniors and kids 3 to 16, free to children under 3. Parking is $7. The park is open daily from 10am to dusk, with extended summer and holiday hours. Call before your visit for specific operating hours.

GUEST SERVICES

Lockers   Lockers are available at the Marketplace for $3 per day ($2 key deposit required).

Strollers & Wheelchairs   Single and double strollers are available for rent at the Marketplace; prices are $6/$12 per day, and a $2 deposit is required. Wheelchairs can be rented for $8 a day (plus $2 deposit); electric wheelchairs are $30 a day.

Kennels   Located at the Park entrance, kennels are available for free on a first-come, first-serve basis. A $15 dollar refundable deposit is required.

Loaner Cameras   Even if you brought your own, you might want to consider taking advantage of LEGOLAND's loaner Polaroid cameras for instant pictures while you tour the park. They're lent for free, on a first-come, first-served basis—film purchase is required to receive the camera.

TOURING THE PARK

A monument to the world's most famous plastic building blocks, LEGOLAND (opened in 1999) is the third such theme park; the branches in Denmark and Britain have proven enormously successful.

While the park's official guidelines imply its attraction is geared toward children of all ages, we think the average MTV- and Playstation-seasoned kid over 10 will find it kind of a snooze. Don't be afraid your toddler is too young, though . . . there'll be plenty for him or her to do. One last note on age—it may be "a country just for kids," but the sheer artistry of construction (especially Miniland, see below) can be enthralling for adults, too.

Below we've listed the park's major areas and most notable rides, attractions, and shows. Because our space is limited—but the variety of small-scale entertainments at LEGOLAND seems endless—please remember this is only a sampling of what the park has to offer.

THE LAKE

Near the park's entrance, this 1¾-acre manmade lake was designed with fish and aquatic plants that create a self-sustaining bio-system.

Coast Cruise 👤   This short, narrated lake tour covers the water-front portion of the park, including an offshore look at Miniland.

IMAGINATION ZONE

The Zone is an interactive workshop for kids of all ages, with demonstration LEGO software, miniature car racing, DUPLO building areas for smaller children, and a splashy power-ski water ride. In the LEGO Show Place Theater, *Taking the World by Storm* is a fun and loud look at scientific experiments with a fun twist.

Mindstorms Learning Center 𝄐𝄐𝄐 One of LEGOLAND's highlights, this 45-minute program uses technology to introduce participants to the world of robotics using the "intelligent" LEGO brick, the RCX, which allows players to create behavioral programs for their robotic pieces. This workshop is targeted to children ages 8 and older who will use LEGO TECHNIC models and control them via computer. Parents are urged to join in—and to make reservations for Mindstorms early in the day, since sessions book up quickly.

MINILAND 𝄐𝄐𝄐

Possibly the most intriguing attraction in the park, this section is dominated by the extraordinary detail of **Miniland U.S.A.,** where landmark scenes from across the United States are replicated with 20 million LEGO bricks in a 1:20 scale. From California we see beachside piers, the Hollywood Bowl, the San Francisco Bay Area, and more; a charming New England Harbor features gray clapboard houses, fishing wharfs, and electric trains that run between the harbor and the countryside, where animated LEGO livestock moves at the touch of a button; the colorful New Orleans section features an endlessly festive Mardi Gras jazz parade plus antebellum mansions and riverfront paddle steamers; and the spectacular New York City faithfully recreates the Manhattan skyline, Central Park, and a cutaway look at the underground subway—with real moving trains. Adults might recognize most of what they're seeing, but a guided mini-tour (see posted tour times in the entry plaza) will fill in the blanks and help educate younger visitors.

CASTLE HILL

Home to the park's most popular rides, this medieval themed play area also offers jousting, rope climbs, mazes, and slide adventures for kids. In the Courtyard Theatre, *Medieval Merriment* is a corny but fun show that enlists youngsters in the audience to help rescue the dragon trapped in the castle.

The Dragon This relatively tame (height restriction: 42") roller coaster sweeps through Castle Hill and even into the Castle itself, where medieval scenes are constructed entirely from LEGO bricks.

Spellbreaker 🎠   LEGOLAND's newest attraction lures riders with a friendly witch; once under her spell, riders are hoisted up a tower then released to race in midair, suspended from an overhead track. Fans of Harry Potter won't be able to resist this one!

FUN TOWN

Here's where kids can play at being grown-ups, experimenting with driving cars, flying airplanes and helicopters, and piloting speedboats. On the Fun Town Stage, *The Big Test* is a charming, funny, and wacky stunt show that teaches fire safety as it entertains.

Driving School 🎠🎠   This kid-powered ride gives kids 6 to 13 a brief course in driving safety and the rules of the road, then are let loose in LEGO cars on a test course where they actually control the vehicle (no rails). Ample seating surrounding the course provides a place for parents to take a break while watching children test their driving skills. There's also an easy version for kids 3 to 5 called **Junior Driving School.**

Skipper School   As in the driving school, children—and adults—can maneuver their own LEGO boat in an isolated part of the lake.

VILLAGE GREEN 🎠

Using DUPLO bricks scaled for the littlest LEGO users, this village is a whimsical garden—a comfortable, secure space with secrets and surprises to delight a young child. Small-scale rides include **Fairy Tale Brook,** a boat ride past classic storybook characters; **Safari Trek,** a jeep ride to see all-LEGO wild beasts; a gentle DUPLO train that makes a simple loop; and **Water Works,** a water-themed playground where kids activate a musical water fountain by jumping on cushioned keypads (those that get splashed can stand in front of giant dryers). Live shows in the Village Green range from a dinosaur excavation adventure story to a short magic trick demonstration and even a sing-a-long with **Joel the Singing Cowboy.**

THE RIDGE

This overlook orientation point offers panoramic views of the park from its two rides: the Sky Cycle (see below) and the **Kid Power Tower,** where riders hoist themselves up for a birds-eye view.

Sky Cycle 🎠🎠🎠   You can see this unique and colorful ride—high atop a track on the Ridge—upon entering the park. It's one of the most popular (and subject to long lines), where pedal-powered (that means you!) cars travel around a panoramic track.

WHERE TO STAY

Beach Terrace Inn   At Carlsbad's only beachside hostelry (others are across the road or a little farther away), the rooms and the swimming pool/whirlpool all have ocean views. This downtown Best Western property also has a helpful staff. Rooms, although not elegant, are extra large, and some have balconies, fireplaces, and kitchenettes. Suites have separate living rooms and bedrooms. VCRs and videos are available at the front desk. This is a good place for families. You can walk everywhere from here—except LEGOLAND, which is a 5-minute drive away.

2775 Ocean St., Carlsbad, CA 92003. ⓒ **800/433-5415** outside Calif., 800/622-3224 in Calif., or 760/729-5951. Fax 760/729-1078. www.beachterraceinn.com. 49 units. Summer $129–$299 double; from $154 suite. Off-season $119–$209 double; from $134 suite. Extra person $20. Rates include continental breakfast. AE, DC, DISC, MC, V. Free parking. **Amenities:** Outdoor pool, whirlpool; self-service laundry; dry cleaning. *In room:* A/C, TV w/pay movies, dataport, fridge, coffeemaker, hairdryer, iron, safe.

Pelican Cove Inn   This Cape Cod-style hideaway 2 blocks from the beach, combines romance with luxury. Hosts Kris and Nancy Nayudu see to your every need, from furnishing guest rooms with feather beds and down comforters to providing beach chairs and towels or preparing a picnic basket (with 24 hours' notice). Each room features a fireplace and private entrance; some have private spa tubs. The airy La Jolla room is loveliest, with bay windows and a cupola ceiling. Breakfast can be enjoyed in the garden if weather permits. Courtesy transportation from the Oceanside train station is available.

320 Walnut Ave., Carlsbad, CA 92008. ⓒ **888/PEL-COVE** or 760/434-5995. www.pelican-cove.com. 8 units. $90–$180 double. Rates include full breakfast. Extra person $15. Midweek and seasonal discounts available. AE, MC, V. Free parking. From downtown Carlsbad, follow Carlsbad Blvd. south to Walnut Ave.; turn left and drive 2½ blocks. *In room:* TV, no phone.

Tamarack Beach Resort   This resort property's rooms, in the village across the street from the beach, are restfully decorated with beachy wicker furniture. Fully equipped suites have stereos, full kitchens, washers, and dryers. The pretty Tamarack has a pleasant lobby and a sunny pool courtyard with barbecue grills. Dini's by the Sea is a good restaurant that is popular with locals.

3200 Carlsbad Blvd., Carlsbad, CA 92008. ⓒ **800/334-2199** or 760/729-3500. Fax 760/434-5942. www.tamarackresort.com. 77 units. $140–$215 double; $210–$340 suite. Children 12 and under stay free in parents' room. Off season discounts and weekly rates available. Rates include continental breakfast.

AE, MC, V. Free underground parking. **Amenities:** Restaurant; outdoor pool; 2 whirlpools; exercise room. *In room:* A/C, TV/VCR w/complimentary movie library, fridge, coffeemaker.

WHERE TO DINE

There are conveniently located snack stands and quick meal spots throughout LEGOLAND, in addition to three sit-down restaurants (two of which offer birthday party services). **Fun Town Market** is a cafeteria-style restaurant with separate stands for different courses (salad bar, pasta station, rotisserie chicken, bakery, and so on); the **Knight's Table** is a barbecue joint offering ribs, husk-roasted corn, rosemary chicken, baked beans, cornbread, and a menu of other choices and traditional accompaniments (including beer and wine); and **Ristorante Brickolini** fires up the wood-burning oven for thin crusted gourmet pizzas, plus a menu of salads and fresh pasta.

Outside the park, Carlsbad's favorite eatery is **Bellefleur Winery & Restaurant,** 5610 Paseo del Norte (✆ **760/603-1919;** www.bellefleur.com), which boasts the "complete wine country experience" although there's no wine country evident among the surrounding outlet mall and car dealerships. But their cavernous semi-industrial dining room, coupled with the wood-fired and wine-enhanced aromas emanating from Bellefleur's clanging open kitchen, somehow evoke the casual yet sophisticated ambiance of California wine-producing regions like Santa Barbara and Napa. This multi-functional space includes a tasting bar and open-air dining patio in addition to the main seating area and a glassed-in barrel aging room. The place can be noisy and spirited, drawing both exhausted shoppers and savvy San Diegans for a cuisine that incorporates North County's abundant produce with fresh fish and meats. Lunchtime sandwiches and salads surpass the shopping-mall standard, while dinner choices feature oak-grilled beef tenderloin or Colorado rack of lamb, mashed potatoes enhanced with garlic, horseradish, or olive *tapenade,* and rich reduction sauces of premium balsamic vinegar, wild mushroom demi-glacé, or sweet-tart tamarind. The restaurant is moderately priced, and open for lunch and dinner daily.

Index

See also Accommodations and Restaurant indexes, below.

FROMMER'S® COMPLETE TRAVEL GUIDES

Alaska
Amsterdam
Argentina & Chile
Arizona
Atlanta
Australia
Austria
Bahamas
Barcelona, Madrid & Seville
Beijing
Belgium, Holland & Luxembourg
Bermuda
Boston
British Columbia & the Canadian
  Rockies
Budapest & the Best of Hungary
California
Canada
Cancún, Cozumel & the Yucatán
Cape Cod, Nantucket &
  Martha's Vineyard
Caribbean
Caribbean Cruises & Ports of Call
Caribbean Ports of Call
Carolinas & Georgia
Chicago
China
Colorado
Costa Rica
Denmark
Denver, Boulder & Colorado Springs
England
Europe
European Cruises & Ports of Call
Florida
France

Germany
Great Britain
Greece
Greek Islands
Hawaii
Hong Kong
Honolulu, Waikiki & Oahu
Ireland
Israel
Italy
Jamaica
Japan
Las Vegas
London
Los Angeles
Maryland & Delaware
Maui
Mexico
Montana & Wyoming
Montréal & Québec City
Munich & the Bavarian Alps
Nashville & Memphis
Nepal
New England
New Mexico
New Orleans
New York City
New Zealand
Nova Scotia, New Brunswick &
  Prince Edward Island
Oregon
Paris
Philadelphia & the Amish Country
Portugal
Prague & the Best of the Czech
  Republic

Provence & the Riviera
Puerto Rico
Rome
San Antonio & Austin
San Diego
San Francisco
Santa Fe, Taos & Albuquerque
Scandinavia
Scotland
Seattle & Portland
Shanghai
Singapore & Malaysia
South Africa
South America
Southeast Asia
South Florida
South Pacific
Spain
Sweden
Switzerland
Texas
Thailand
Tokyo
Toronto
Tuscany & Umbria
USA
Utah
Vancouver & Victoria
Vermont, New Hampshire
  & Maine
Vienna & the Danube Valley
Virgin Islands
Virginia
Walt Disney World & Orlando
Washington, D.C.
Washington State

FROMMER'S® DOLLAR-A-DAY GUIDES

Australia from $50 a Day
California from $70 a Day
Caribbean from $70 a Day
England from $75 a Day
Europe from $70 a Day

Florida from $70 a Day
Hawaii from $80 a Day
Ireland from $60 a Day
Italy from $70 a Day
London from $85 a Day

New York from $90 a Day
Paris from $80 a Day
San Francisco from $70 a Day
Washington, D.C., from $80
  a Day

FROMMER'S® PORTABLE GUIDES

Acapulco, Ixtapa & Zihuatanejo
Alaska Cruises & Ports of Call
Amsterdam
Aruba
Australia's Great Barrier Reef
Bahamas
Baja & Los Cabos
Berlin
Big Island of Hawaii
Boston
California Wine Country
Cancún
Charleston & Savannah
Chicago
Disneyland

Dublin
Florence
Frankfurt
Hong Kong
Houston
Las Vegas
London
Los Angeles
Maine Coast
Maui
Miami
New Orleans
New York City
Paris

Phoenix & Scottsdale
Portland
Puerto Rico
Puerto Vallarta, Manzanillo &
  Guadalajara
San Diego
San Francisco
Seattle
Sydney
Tampa & St. Petersburg
Vancouver
Venice
Virgin Islands
Washington, D.C.

FROMMER'S® NATIONAL PARK GUIDES

Family Vacations in the National
  Parks
Grand Canyon

National Parks of the American
  West
Rocky Mountain
Yellowstone & Grand Teton

Yosemite & Sequoia/
  Kings Canyon
Zion & Bryce Canyon

FROMMER'S® MEMORABLE WALKS

Chicago	New York	San Francisco
London	Paris	

FROMMER'S® GREAT OUTDOOR GUIDES

Arizona & New Mexico	Northern California	Vermont & New Hampshire
New England	Southern New England	

SUZY GERSHMAN'S BORN TO SHOP GUIDES

Born to Shop: France	Born to Shop: Italy	Born to Shop: New York
Born to Shop: Hong Kong, Shanghai & Beijing	Born to Shop: London	Born to Shop: Paris

FROMMER'S® IRREVERENT GUIDES

Amsterdam	Los Angeles	San Francisco
Boston	Manhattan	Seattle & Portland
Chicago	New Orleans	Vancouver
Las Vegas	Paris	Walt Disney World
London	Rome	Washington, D.C.

FROMMER'S® BEST-LOVED DRIVING TOURS

Britain	Germany	New England
California	Ireland	Scotland
Florida	Italy	Spain
France		

HANGING OUT™ GUIDES

Hanging Out in England	Hanging Out in France	Hanging Out in Italy
Hanging Out in Europe	Hanging Out in Ireland	Hanging Out in Spain

THE UNOFFICIAL GUIDES®

Bed & Breakfasts and Country Inns in:	Florida with Kids	New Orleans
California	Golf Vacations in the Eastern U.S.	New York City
New England	The Great Smokey & Blue Ridge Mountains	Paris
Northwest		San Francisco
Rockies	Inside Disney	Skiing in the West
Southeast	Hawaii	Southeast with Kids
Beyond Disney	Las Vegas	Walt Disney World
Branson, Missouri	London	Walt Disney World for Grown-ups
California with Kids	Mid-Atlantic with Kids	Walt Disney World for Kids
Chicago	Mini Las Vegas	Washington, D.C.
Cruises	Mini-Mickey	World's Best Diving Vacations
Disneyland	New England & New York with Kids	

SPECIAL-INTEREST TITLES

Frommer's Adventure Guide to Australia & New Zealand	Frommer's Exploring America by RV
	Frommer's Gay & Lesbian Europe
Frommer's Adventure Guide to Central America	Frommer's The Moon
Frommer's Adventure Guide to India & Pakistan	Frommer's New York City with Kids
Frommer's Adventure Guide to South America	Frommer's Road Atlas Britain
Frommer's Adventure Guide to Southeast Asia	Frommer's Road Atlas Europe
Frommer's Adventure Guide to Southern Africa	Frommer's Washington, D.C., with Kids
Frommer's Britain's Best Bed & Breakfasts and Country Inns	Frommer's What the Airlines Never Tell You
	Israel Past & Present
Frommer's France's Best Bed & Breakfasts and Country Inns	The New York Times' Guide to Unforgettable Weekends
Frommer's Italy's Best Bed & Breakfasts and Country Inns	Places Rated Almanac
	Retirement Places Rated
Frommer's Caribbean Hideaways	